gifts 9

HOLY SPIRIT
Revelation & Revolution
EXPLORING HOLY SPIRIT DIMENSIONS

D1052885

REINHARD BONNKE

HOLY SPIRIT
Revelation & Revolution

Exploring Holy Spirit Dimensions

REINHARD BONNKE
WITH GEORGE CANTY

*This book describes
how the Third Person of the Trinity,
the Eternal Spirit of God,
has come into his own this century and
how we came to know his work and identity.*

HOLY SPIRIT
Revelation & Revolution

Reinhard Bonnke with George Canty
English

Copyright © E-R Productions LLC 2007
ISBN 978-1-933106-62-5

Edition 1, Printing 1
7,500 copies

Cover Design: Brand Navigation, U.S.A.
Typeset: Roland Senkel
Photographs: Rob Birkbeck
Oleksandr Volyk
Photo Pages: Carolina Blanco

E-R Productions LLC
P.O. Box 593647
Orlando, Florida 32859
U.S.A.

www.e-r-productions.com

Printed in Singapore

CONTENTS

Credo 7

Foreword 9

CHAPTER 1   Who is the Holy Spirit? 15

CHAPTER 2   The Spirit and His distinctive Work 23

CHAPTER 3   Amazing Grace and the Holy Spirit 27

CHAPTER 4   The Baptism in the Holy Spirit 35

CHAPTER 5   "Times of refreshing shall come from the Lord." 51

CHAPTER 6   Holy Spirit Fire and Passion 55

CHAPTER 7   The Story of the Holy Spirit Movement 65

CHAPTER 8   The Paraclete 69

CHAPTER 9   The Christ of the Spirit 79

CHAPTER 10   Speaking in Tongues 89

CHAPTER 11   New Encounter 107

CHAPTER 12   When the Spirit moves 115

CHAPTER 13   Practice in the Spirit 125

CHAPTER 14   Eagerly desire spiritual Gifts? 135

CHAPTER 15   What are the "Gifts"? 145

God is pouring out his Spirit, manifest power, the greatest non-scientific power on earth.

The Spirit is the creator and upholder of the whole universe and this world is his special interest and responsibility.

Sent by the Father, the Holy Spirit imparts himself to all who believe. No one else can impart him. He is a Person, not a commodity. We cannot order Deity.

The Baptism in the Spirit is physical and spiritual. The Spirit "abides" and makes us aware of his constant presence with assurance of his lasting power.

The Holy Spirit is the Spirit of love, love's beginning and source. Love is shed in our hearts by the Holy Spirit, our greatest asset, mightier than miracles.

The Holy Spirit is the reality of Christianity. Without the Spirit the Christian faith is powerless and impossible. He is the essence, the secret dynamic of the faith, and its actuating force.

The Spirit is the *pneuma*, rushing wind, always active. There is no still wind and no still Holy Spirit. If we claim to have the Spirit we shall be active with him and to that degree. His only instruments are believers.

The Spirit made all things and keeps them together. He cannot care for the world without miracles. To deny miracles is to deny the creator his rights.

One hundred years ago a new age of the Holy Spirit dawned. A new dynamism has since animated hundreds of millions of Christians. It has taken time to impact the world. But what an impact! It is the primary phenomenon in history.

The UK evangelical magazine IDEA[1] quotes David Martin, Emeritus Professor of Sociology at the London School of Economics, as saying that the Holy Spirit movement in the last century "is the most dramatic development of Christianity in the century recently concluded." Harvey Cox, Professor of Divinity at Harvard has called it "the reshaping of religion in the 21st century."[2]

It has been claimed that greater advances have been made in understanding the Spirit – the theology – since 1900 than in the previous 1,900 years. This may well be the case. We know nothing about God unless the Spirit reveals it. Jesus said the Spirit would speak not about himself but about the Son: *"He, the Spirit of truth, will bring glory to me by taking what is mine and making it known to you"* (John 16:13-14).

The swing of interest in the Spirit came from the fringe, from unknown faith people, not from scholars, though it has produced scholars. Such people – nobodies, coming full of the Spirit from the outer edges of Christianity, were met with suspicion, as one would expect. They had only experience, and to men of the Church no theology meant no credentials, no bona fides.

---

[1] IDEA July/August 2006 from Jerusalem to Azusa Street
[2] Harvey Cox, The Reshaping of Religion in the 21st Century, da capo Press ©1995 Harvey Cox

Yet, if the Church was demanding a theology of the Spirit, why wasn't it providing one? Where was the Church's theology of the Ascension? Where were the guides to the Holy Spirit in action? It looked suspiciously as if Holy Spirit miracle Christianity, the standard and original faith of the New Testament, was expected never to be seen again. With the Holy Spirit in action New Testament religion could become common experience once more.

However, was there anyone who could still imagine what first century Christianity was like, what the 120 disciples were like on the day of Pentecost? Well, hundreds of millions of people around the world today speak of their experience as a repeat of apostolic times. Today's worldwide Holy Spirit effects may have previously been beyond people's imaginations, but they are obviously real and cannot be ignored.

We shall always be learning about God. That will be one of our eternal joys. Jesus promised that the Spirit would guide us into all truth – guide us, not jettison us into a mass of truth like a bullet into the Swiss mountains. He said he had things to tell his disciples, but they were not ready for them. Isaiah said God had to teach people *"rule on rule, rule on rule, a little here, a little there"* (Isaiah 28:10).

Today we are learning even more of the Spirit. The original group of "discoverers" shone with a light that reached Europe from a half-burnt-down mission hall on Azusa Street in 1906. They had little teaching on the Spirit in their own churches and certainly no scholarship. So they picked up their Bibles to teach themselves. Scholarship is not needed for a walk with God. Those Spirit-baptized fathers bequeathed to us some basic teaching that is still important today, a century later. Daniel was told that *"knowledge shall increase"* (Daniel 12:4, NKJV) and we do, indeed, understand more as time goes on. Bible revelations filter through only gradually until they become the general teaching of the church. It may take decades, even centuries, before a truth becomes the currency of common belief. We can see that as we look back across the centuries of church history.

Things said in this book are likely to be new insights to many. These are not trivial matters; they are Bible truths and therefore potent. Nor are they the *"great matters or things too wonderful for me"* that the Psalmist preferred to leave alone (Psalm 131:1). Unfortunately, there are people around today who think that most of the Bible belongs to that category. Charles Spurgeon said that some high-flown teachers think that Jesus said, "Feed my giraffes," putting the food of the Word far out of reach of normal creatures. These chapters are a suitable diet for all, including "babes in Christ." The apostle Paul found that the pagans of Athens were hungry for philosophical novelties, not truth, and the Areopagus institute was there to examine them. Jesus had different ideas: *"Every teacher of the law who has been instructed about the kingdom of heaven is like the owner of a house who brings out of his storeroom new treasures as well as old"* (Matthew 13:52). We can all walk with God with understanding, though we learn slowly and do not jump into new shoes every day.

Holy Spirit-filled churches have changed tremendously this century, but the Word of God is still the floor plan. Earlier Spirit-filled people lived through stormy waters. It was the Word that made them what they were; the Word was the unshakeable rock on which they built, not experience alone, as this book will show.

It is the duty of those who teach to strengthen Christian basics and to provide evidence of the new life produced by the living Word.

A Fuller College professor stated that this Holy Spirit revival "is a profound augmentation of all Christian teaching." It is the Holy Spirit who adds depth to every major doctrine. The revolutionary secret is out: The gospel is for the body as well as the soul. God is as active on earth as he is in heaven. We know now who the Holy Spirit really is. He is the agent of divine action on earth.

Of course, there is always the periphery, the zealous but not wise, the arrogant who claim superior private revelations, and those who suppose that having the Spirit guarantees that God must do whatever they say. New schemes, panaceas, gimmicks, revivalist and instant church-filling and church-growth "secrets" come to us as if from a production belt, together with private instructions and directives personally from the Almighty. But extremists are not our role models.

Tens of millions of people today are filled with the Holy Spirit, creating an acute need for teaching. The experience of the Spirit is wonderful, but we must grow. I longed for an up-to-date guide of dependable authority so believers could see from the Word what are acceptable practice and standards. This little book is an attempt in that direction. Our campaigns and the many people involved have made such a guide urgent.

I am publishing this book with the support of well-qualified Christian scholars. An English friend, George Canty, who also longed for such a book, joined in. That we were both looking for the same thing seemed to me more than coincidence; we took it as divine prompting. George Canty has unique qualifications, having had a real Acts 2 experience as long ago as 1926; today, still drawing on the power of it, he continues to play an active part in a wide range of gospel initiatives. He is a Bible theologian with a clear and original mind.

The Holy Spirit is the inspiring Spirit. These chapters are just one result, hopefully written in terms that everyone can enjoy. It is not a re-hash of things everybody knows, nor is it padded out with dramatized "comfort writing." This is original and fresh Bible teaching. I have asked for God's anointing on this volume and that the Holy Spirit, the Great Interpreter, will anoint the minds and hearts of all readers.

Testimony

When a boy, I longed for the baptism in the Spirit more than for my daily bread. My father eventually took me to a place where a noted preacher was holding services. While there, with no one near me, I felt as if all heaven was cramming into my soul. Filled with God, I found myself speaking in tongues. A spiritual instinct was born in me, prompting me, inspiring me, and leading me. I don't need to pray for God's presence, I don't seek him. I simply rely on his promise. We are his temples. He is where we are and he will never leave or forsake us. The Spirit of God performs his wonders.

The Holy Spirit comes

for the best and for the worst of us,

the Father's promise sent by the Son.

What a gift!

CHAPTER 1

Who is the Holy Spirit?

Throughout most of the church's history the Holy Spirit was not much more than a name. The immediate answer to the question used as the title of this chapter is that the Holy Spirit is God in action on earth.

For centuries people thought of the "Holy Ghost" as just that, a holy ghost, a sort of religious fragrance or ambience lingering in Gothic churches. The majesty of the Almighty, the Third Person of the Godhead, seemed known only as a mysterious cathedral atmosphere. That is quite a status reduction!

To talk about him we have first to identify him. He is the power of Pentecost. He began the Christian Church. We can pinpoint when and where this happened. It was in AD 29 at the annual Jewish festival held 50 days after Christ's crucifixion, called the day of Pentecost. That morning the Spirit of God burst upon the world in reality, not as a sweet influence but literally as a hurricane. He announced his own arrival with the miracle of 120 disciples speaking in tongues. This noisy outburst attracted the first Christian congregation.

He did not come just to demonstrate divine things, to provide a one-off experience that people could remember when they grew old.

The disciples were emboldened. They cast aside timidity and challenged the world. For many thousands of years, no matter where you look, mankind lived entrenched in superstitions and traditions. In AD 29 those people in an obscure corner of the world became bigger than life size, ready to challenge the devil, the world, and history itself. The well-known evangelist Smith Wigglesworth said the Acts of the Apostles was written because the apostles acted.

This was the new living resource promised by Christ. He had risen to God and sent the evidence of it, the gift of the Spirit. Seated at the right hand of the heavenly throne, he gave the world physical proof of it. The disciples experienced something that had never been known on earth before.

Despite such tangible experience, as memories of the apostles dimmed, the Holy Spirit somehow became a remote presence. Jesus was remembered, and so were all his works; as time went by a great Christian statement was written about him, the Apostles' Creed. That creed has been recited on fifty thousand Sundays by millions of Christians. Yet it made only passing mention of the Holy Spirit – "I believe in the Holy Spirit." We do not know who wrote the Creed, but it was certainly not the Apostles. Whoever composed it was evidently not as conscious of the Holy Spirit and his role in affairs as the first disciples.[1]

The original version of the all-important Nicene Creed (AD 325) merely named the Holy Spirit. The Council of Constantinople (AD 553) added that he is the Lord and giver of life, proceeding from the Father and the Son and that he is to be worshiped and glorified together with the Father and Son. The Council of Toledo (AD 589) only spoke of the Holy Spirit as proceeding from the Father and Son, not of his work. The second Council of Constantinople names the Spirit only once and the third Council Statement of Faith does not mention the Holy Spirit. Even the 28 Lutheran Articles of Faith and Doctrine give no details about the Spirit. The 25 Canons of the Council of Orange make only a passing reference to the Spirit and attributes the work of the Spirit to "grace."

Dr. Arthur Headlam, a former Bishop of Gloucester, said in his commentary that it was not understood what the Holy Spirit gifts were that were exercised in the early church. However, Paul wrote to the Galatians as if the Holy Spirit experience was a normal part of everyday life: *"We live by the Spirit"* (Galatians 5:25). The great Bible translator J. B. Lightfoot knew little of the Spirit himself, saying that to live by the Spirit was "an ideal rather than an actual life." This seemed to have been the accepted situation by the late 19th century. Holy Spirit reality had drifted out of sight.

> The Holy Spirit is God in action on earth.

The Spirit is God, and God is not remote. That was never his intention. We ought to know him as much as we know the Father and Jesus. The Father and the Son are one, but also can be distinguished. We recognize their roles. What is the role of the Spirit, his distinguishing feature?

The Holy Spirit is the Third Person of the Trinity at work on earth. Everything that God does here, outside of heaven, is by the Spirit. All the experience of believers, forgiveness, answers to prayer, assurance, joy, healings and signs are the works of God performed by the Holy Spirit. Today God is at work around us through the Holy Spirit. We learn who the Spirit is in the New Testament. For instance, the whole book of the Acts of the Apostles has been called "The Acts of the Holy Spirit."

> The Holy Spirit is the Third Person of the Trinity at work on earth. Everything that God does here, outside of heaven, is by the Spirit.

The basic Bible truth is that God makes himself known by action, not so much verbally. The Holy Spirit is action. He is the wind from heaven, which is always moving or it would not exist. If we know the Spirit, we know God and we can all know him, just as we know Jesus.

The Holy Spirit is the wonderful resource promised by Jesus. Before then the Spirit was not truly known. The first disciples needed to learn the new potential. The book of Acts is the story of their exploration of the Holy Spirit. They had been sent by Jesus to perform an impossible task, to carry the gospel into the heathen world and to shed light in its thick darkness. They were only fishermen and peasants, but the Holy Spirit made them spiritual giants still honored some 2,000 years later. That is the Holy Spirit. The Holy Spirit is the God of Pentecost, the Spirit of activity, power, love, strength and miracles.

The Holy Spirit has not come to create a cozy atmosphere in a church. We do not draw him into our services by creating the right atmosphere, regardless of whether that is quiet and subdued or noisy and exuberant. The Holy Spirit does not need to be attracted, invoked, persuaded or baited. He is not a reluctant or indifferent visitor but, following his own will and desire, he comes to take up residence.

The apostles were not praying for the Spirit, but he came, invaded the place; any atmosphere they might have experienced together was blown away, invaded by a *"rushing mighty wind"* (Acts 2:2, NKV). The Spirit is the atmosphere of heaven itself and heaven comes down here with him. He is the pneuma, the wind of heaven blowing through our stuffy traditions and stagnation.

We may sing "Welcome, welcome, Holy Spirit", but he does not come because of our welcome. He is no guest, no stranger invited in for an hour or two. He is the Lord from heaven and invites us into his presence. Where there is faith and the Word, he finds his natural environment.

The Holy Spirit does not choose the strong and the capable, although he does not ignore them either. However, his purpose is to give strength to the weak and needy, the little folk who think little of themselves. Their weak-

> The Holy Spirit is the God of Pentecost, the Spirit of activity, power, love, strength and miracles.

ness attracts his power, his all-sufficiency and life-giving dynamism. He comes for the best and for the worst of us, the Father's promise sent by the Son. What a gift!

We read with wonder and joy what the Spirit was in Bible days. That is the Spirit we are talking about here. He is the eternal Spirit, no different now than then. In fact the Old Testament days were not his great days. He is the New Testament Spirit. He is the essence of the Christian faith, brought to us by the gospel. There is no Christianity without him. He is not an accessory, but the very substance of what we believe. He is God on earth, actively indwelling and saturating every particle of what we experience. This means that Christianity is a supernatural faith. A non-supernatural gospel is only a shell.

The New Testament contains not a single word suggesting the Spirit would ever withdraw or change. Even if we "quench the Spirit," or "grieve" the Spirit, he does not retreat and leave us. David prayed, *"Do not take your Holy Spirit from me"* (Psalm 51:11), but that was a thousand years before he came to abide with us. Our unbelief grieves the Holy Spirit. We can certainly grieve him by what we do, but we could neither quench nor grieve him unless he was with us. The world cannot quench or grieve him. Only believers have that dubious privilege.

The supreme work of the Spirit is salvation. His priority is not Christians concerned about scruples and finer points of spirituality and holiness. Any virtue of ours is swallowed up, carried away in a wave of his sanctifying presence.

The apostles needed the Spirit and so do we, even more. In Bible times the world had 300 million people, all unevangelized. Today there are almost seven thousand million on earth and most of them are unevangelized. We need to do what the apostles did. If we do, God will give us what he gave them.

The book of the Acts of the Apostles does not portray peak Holy Spirit power, but only what the first disciples did by the Spirit. Nothing is said about it being the maximum of possibility. **There is no maximum.** The early Christians are not our role models. Their story is only a first sampling of the potentialities of Holy Spirit ministry. The field is open to us. Paul prayed *"that the eyes of your heart may be enlightened in order that you may know […] his incomparably great power for us who believe. That power is like the working of his mighty strength, which he exerted in Christ when he raised him from the dead"* (Ephesians 1:18-20).

Christians were never intended to fight the world, the flesh and the devil with only their own resources – whether they lived in the first or the twenty-first century. The gospel is the *"power of God"*

(Romans 1:16) – that is, by the Holy Spirit, but not when we ignore him. How much preaching today sounds as if the preacher had just come out of the upper room with the Apostles? How much sounds as if the gospel really is the power of God? Preachers who talk to their congregations like doctors in their clinic, passionless, give the Holy Spirit no chance. The Christian job cannot be done without the Spirit's anointing and that we know. *"Be filled with the Spirit!"* is our instruction (Ephesians 5:18). Being purpose-driven is part of it, but being Spirit-driven is the New Testament pattern. He is the motivator and the motivating power.

The half million words of the Old Testament is God's treatise on the Holy Spirit. It demonstrates that whole nations tread the road of tragedy if the Spirit of God is ignored. The Spirit touched an individual in Israel only now and then, but otherwise the nation was on a slippery downward slope. When the Spirit came everything changed. It was a supernatural gospel with revolutionary effects.

> We need to do what the apostles did. If we do, God will give us what he gave them.

The faith spread. Over the decades it became decadent and secular, and its history suggests the Christian church has failed to realize the potential of the Spirit. The Spirit has always been at work, for he is the restless, ever-active One. He may have been given little recognition, but he was working against the flow of the corruptions of the Church. The church has been embroiled in intrigues, politics, theological heresies, internecine strife, debates over issues remote from anything Jesus said, and oblivious of the Holy Spirit's reality.

It is high time for us to know who the Holy Spirit is and what
Jesus said about him as the secret of gospel power. It is not a case of
struggling and sweating to get the Spirit, but of letting the Spirit
come in. We do not make his power. We do not make him effective. We do not generate Holy Spirit power by prayer, sweat,
agony, time, effort, good works, or anything else. The Father gives
us the Spirit as a gift, not a reward or wages, something we earn.
If we could make ourselves so good that we deserved the Holy
Spirit, we would not need him. Like Elisha, we are all called to
pick up the Elijah mantle, but our Elijah is Christ Jesus. We do not
ask, *"Where is the God of Elijah?"* (2 Kings 2:14), but "Where is
the God of our Lord Jesus Christ?" for one greater than Elijah has
come.

CHAPTER 2

The Spirit and His distinctive Work

One distinguishing fact about him is given in 1 Peter 1:12. The Holy Spirit is described as the One *"sent from heaven."*

John 13:3 tells us that Jesus came from heaven. *"The Word became flesh and made his dwelling among us"* (Greek *eskeénoosen*, "tabernacled") (John 1:14). What a wonderful thought – God taking up residence with us. It was, in fact, exactly what Jesus promised: *"If anyone loves me [...] my Father will love him, and we will come to him and make our home with him"* (John 14:23). It was true of Jesus but it is true also of the Spirit of Christ: *"The Father will give you another Counselor to be with you for ever"* (John 14:16).

The Holy Spirit is not a rare experience for withdrawn mystics, but the natural expectation of us all. God desires us to desire him. It is his planned wish to come close to us, by his Spirit. That was so from the moment of creation. The Spirit was to be the environment in which we would live and walk daily.

The world regards Spirit-filled people as weird, strange. Yes, to them we are. We are a new race, a new species, new creatures in Christ, no longer just *homo sapiens*, but regenerated by the Spirit, shaped as vessels of the Spirit. We breathe the *pneuma* of God.

Without the Holy Spirit we are not as God visualized us. *"If any-one does not have the Spirit of Christ, he does not belong to Christ"* (Romans 8:9). "Not belonging to Christ" refers to a distortion in the order. We do not fit his hand. Without the Spirit we do not qualify as useful to God, and are rejected for his ultimate purposes. This is frustrating to God. Jesus promised, *"I will ask the Father, and he will give you another Counselor"* (John 14:16). He expressly wants us to have the Spirit, like bread which a father wants to give his children.

The Spirit of God, the Holy Spirit, is the divine power-agency doing the work. Creation is his handiwork. He made all things, heaven and earth, and is active in both spheres. Hebrews 1:3 tells us that the Son is *"sustaining all things by his powerful word."* He is committed. He carries the responsibility of earth and its inhabitants, and no doubt heaven also though the Bible does not actually say so.

> The Holy Spirit is not a rare experience for withdrawn mystics, but the natural expectation of us all. God desires us to desire him.

The Spirit is the author of all things visible and invisible. Miracles are one of a piece with creation and essential to God's control. All things exist by the Holy Spirit. Nothing is more natural than the supernatural. The surprise is not miracles, but no miracles would certainly be a surprise. The Spirit spun the world and all its essences out of his hand. He made them and can remake them, can heal, save, and perform signs and wonders. It is impossible for things to be otherwise. If we can build a house and look after it, so can God!

The first Bible words show us the background situation. *"In the beginning God created the heavens and the earth. Now the earth was formless and empty, darkness was over the surface of the deep and the Spirit of God was hovering over the waters"* (Genesis 1:1-2). He was awaiting the sign to take over. All the splendors of earth, sea and sky were his institution and God appointed him as curator and caretaker. The Holy Spirit brought this world to birth out of the swirling vortex of time and space as from a pregnant universe, the special world where God would wage the final war against evil.

Why should infinite God concentrate such attention on one planet peopled by such a discreditable race? That question brings us to the God who reveals himself to humankind, but wrapped in clouds of his mysterious glory. We stand back in awe when we read, *"God so loved the world"* (John 3:16) – this world, our world, among a trillion other worlds where his Son was not sent to be crucified. Our world is not a pastime to him, not an interesting interlude in eternity watching how free creatures behave. This was the crucial world of eternal issues. Affairs here had to be successful. That is why the Holy Spirit is here. He could trust only the Spirit and his beloved Son.

> We stand back in awe when we read, "God so loved the world" – this world, our world, among a trillion other worlds where his Son was not sent to be crucified.

Whether we realize it or not, we are the subjects of the closest divine attention. To all intents and purposes, Hagar was a reject. But, face to face with the divine messenger, she understood something that is still true today: *"You are the God who sees me"* (Genesis 16:13).

In a Christian meeting, we may sing "Welcome, welcome, Holy Spirit", but welcomed or not, he is there. Indeed, is it somewhat arrogant to welcome him? Whose meeting is it? He welcomes us or there would be no meeting at all. He prepares a table before us – only the heathens prepare a table for their gods. This world is one of God's own "mansions" or dwellings. We are his guests. He is the host.

That is who the Spirit is, and there is more to him than can be written in any single chapter.

CHAPTER 3

Amazing Grace and the Holy Spirit

We learn very slowly, but these are the last days when, as the prophet Daniel heard, *"knowledge shall increase"* (Daniel 12:4, NKJV). Anyone in their nineties must surely have described to their grandchildren how everything has changed, even the culture and pattern of thinking. Tragically, the mind of modern man is generally devoid of the fear of God, so over the centuries we have become not better people and our sins are as old-fashioned as Adam's. At the same time almost every common feature of our homes was unknown 90 years ago.

It is hard for us to imagine that less than 200 years ago the fastest transport was a horse and the only pictures were drawn by hand; there were no photographs, and no TV starring celebrated nobodies. For 10,000 years mankind advanced little until the modern explosion of science and technology. Morally and religiously we learn slowly, hampered by human self-interest. When the first H Bomb was dropped, the newspapers all ran the same cliché to the effect that morals have lagged behind science. As Jesus said, we are *"slow of heart to believe"* (Luke 24:25).

That is definitely the case as far as the Holy Spirit is concerned. He remained shadowy and mysterious for 1,900 years. Salvation was known but the Holy Spirit seemed a stranger even in church. Yet he was at work. All God did here was by the Holy Spirit.

However, theologians and teachers replaced this holy Person by a non-personal power – "grace" – turning what is basically the attitude of God into a force. They believed God – or something doing something, spiritually at least. Spiritual action had to be credited to somewhere. It was not credited to the Holy Spirit but to "grace."

The great teacher Augustine of Hippo, who lived 1,600 years ago, set the teaching of the church for future centuries. His powerful intellect seemed infallible. His salvation scheme was accepted as if written by an angel from God. But Augustine was a philosopher and handled spiritual teaching in the manner of the Aristotelian philosophers. His logic led him into more than one spiritual and doctrinal cul-de-sac.

Augustine, and others before him, worked out his teaching on salvation around the word "grace", but grace is simply God's attitude of loving favor. It is not a separate "thing," but a name for his care for worthless mankind. In Scripture God's favors and gifts are sometimes called his grace, by analogy or figuratively.

Augustine's church beliefs are followed even today in many church circles from Catholic to evangelical. There are popular hymns about grace or to grace, for few people worry about the serious teachings or history behind it. Of course, Scripture tells us about the grace of our Lord Jesus Christ. Jesus was God's supreme act of grace or favor. Jesus was *"full of grace"* (John 1:14) – that is, graciousness. He himself was the embodiment of God's favor towards us. He was God's love gift, his way of showing that he was reconciled to sinful men and women. He in a wonderful sense was grace, but grace was not a mysterious faceless element moving irresistibly among believers.

In older teaching, grace did everything God might do? People spoke of "sovereign grace" as if it were an independent power with a will of its own. The 18th century song of John Newton *Amazing Grace* is found in most hymn books and credits everything to grace. It does not name God or Christ. That may be why non-church people and even non-believers use it so often at funerals and weddings. Grace was not someone to pray to or worship. "Sovereign grace"

> Being of God, this power, coming through the baptism in the Spirit with speaking in tongues, became the lever of change.

chose who would be saved. "Classic" revival theory saw grace at work choosing and making up the number of the elect, "saved by grace alone."

Spirit-filled believers today recognize the wonderful grace of God, but it is not seen as an energy or operating force. All spiritual action is by the Holy Spirit. Jesus is the one who saves – and not by proxy using some other entity to do his work. The Holy Spirit takes of the things of Christ and applies them to our need.

In Catholic thought, grace could be generated and accumulated. Sacrifice and total devotion created grace and made a saint. For ordinary Christians there were "the means of grace" – prayers, sacraments, and church attendance. People were said to be "in a state of grace" if they had perhaps just been to confession. Grace was spiritual currency, earned by work. There were some very holy characters who had acquired a surplus of grace and could share their store of grace with others. Such outstanding people usually had afflicted themselves with extreme severities and deprivations. They were the men and women the Church "canonized" as "saints." There are patron saints of countries and others with various special interests to help the living. St. Jude is very popular at present.

We are not concerned here with the truth or untruth of that practice. We refer to it only to show how "grace" was a central issue for some 1,600 years. Then, in 1904, a much spoken-of "revival" broke out in Wales under Evan Roberts. He traveled around southern Wales, having been baptized in the Holy Spirit. He was a pioneer, relying on the Holy Spirit as he moved from chapel to chapel preaching repentance and salvation. The Welsh revival was maybe the first to be recognized as a Holy Spirit revival and not a "grace" revival. God began to break through from the "grace" theory of the past. Christian leaders spoke of the "power" present, and recognized it as the same power as was evident in the early Spirit-anointed meetings in Los Angeles.

Being of God, this power, coming through the baptism in the Spirit with speaking in tongues, became the lever of change. In an old Methodist building in Azusa Street, Los Angeles, God was again using the weak things of this world to confound the mighty. A score or so of simple Christian believers knew the "secret" and enjoyed a true Acts of the Apostles blessing. Teachings of the past received a make-over. The Holy Spirit showed his hand and there was no mistaking it. A later chapter will look more closely at that episode (chapter 7).

Let us pause for a moment to look at the word "grace" (Greek *charis*). It is an expression mainly used by Paul – over 100 times, in fact. He speaks of it as God's attitude of favor towards us, undeserved and unsolicited. Jesus did not use the word. Paul spoke of it figuratively but not as something existing in its own right. There simply is no active divine force except the Holy Spirit. All credit, all glory for divine action must be given to him, not to some other independent force called "grace." *"There is no power but of God"* (Romans 13:1, KJV). No other powers or divine emanations exist beside the Holy Spirit. Kingdom power, "praise power," "prayer power," – if any are real, it is all the operation of the Holy Spirit. Mary was visited by the angel Gabriel and was told that she was *"highly favored,"* that is, "graced" (Luke 1:28), but Gabriel said she would become the mother of Jesus by the *"power of the Most High"* (Luke 1:35) – not by grace.

God performs nothing by an impersonal power. The reality of the Spirit is him, and we can walk in the Spirit and enjoy the knowledge of the Spirit. This has been written in Scripture all along. Christ himself worked his wonders by the Holy Spirit. The book of Acts teaches us total dependence on the Holy Spirit and says that *"God anointed Jesus of Nazareth with the Holy Spirit and power, and he went around doing good and healing all who were under the power of the devil"* (Acts 10:38).

> It is tremendous to realize that whatever God does, the whole Godhead does with equal interest.

Jesus himself told us that he did what the Father did and it was by the Holy Spirit. The Holy Spirit is the operator carrying out the will of the Father at the Word of the Son. The Son is the Executor of the Father and the Spirit is the Executor of the Son. Jesus said *"I do always the things which the Father does"* – that is by the Spirit (John 5:19).

It is tremendous to realize that whatever God does, the whole Godhead does with equal interest. Everything that God is, is behind our Christian experience. Jesus saves us by the Father's love and the Spirit. All God's work, all Christ's work is implemented by Holy Spirit action in us. The Spirit takes the work of Christ, his death and resurrection, and transfers it, implements it, and makes it effective in all believers. By the Holy Spirit we identify with Christ and he identifies with us in all his saving glory and grace. The Spirit within us is active, not latent. He "abides." He is in residence. He affects every human department, physical, spiritual and psychological. He is our empowering strength for witness, so that all we are conveys the truth, not only by miracles but by a Spirit-filled life. It all starts when we come to know Jesus – which is made possible by the Holy Spirit.

The Holy Spirit is God's gift to us to carry out his work in this world. Some think only in spiritual or heavenly terms; their gospel has no physical or miracle side. Prayer is often made by people who believe miracles were only for apostolic times; yet an answer to their prayers would involve the miraculous. It is part of human nature to pray to God for help, even when people do not believe in miracles. We cannot get away from the fact that the gospel is for heaven and earth.

Scripture says *"John did no miracle"* (John 10:41, KJV), for the Spirit had not yet been given. John himself proclaimed that the One coming would baptize with the Holy Spirit and with fire (Luke 3:16). Jesus came and astonished even John with mighty signs and deeds. Our gospel is not a John the Baptist gospel, a water-baptism gospel, but Christ's fire of the Holy Spirit gospel.

Unless we give the Holy Spirit his place in our teaching we make nonsense of the whole divine scheme. The Spirit is the Maker of the whole order, heaven and earth, all things visible or invisible. Those who limit the Spirit to the heavenly realm or unseen spiritual effects are shutting the Holy Spirit out from his own world.

God put us under the active care of the Holy Spirit from the day of creation, right through all time, in Christ. He is our very present and immediate God, devoted to the heirs of salvation and to ensuring that our work and way in the world lead to God's eternal glory.

Unless we give the Holy Spirit his place in our teaching we make nonsense of the whole divine scheme.

The Holy Spirit rests not only

on the whole spiritual temple,

but occupies the heart of every believer.

We are the shrine of the Holy Spirit:

"If anyone does not have the Spirit of Christ,

he does not belong to Christ"

CHAPTER 4

The Baptism in the Holy Spirit

Part 1

The Bible does not deal with problems and explanations. It cuts the Gordian knot with the sword of experience.

Baptism in the Spirit is real. In sacramental ritual a priest may pronounce that a candidate receives the Holy Spirit, but that is not quite the same as the wind, fire, and tongues of Acts chapter 2!

When Pentecostals first came on the scene and were opposed, a new theory was invented: that the whole church was baptized in the Spirit on the day of Pentecost, once for all and for ever. That "baptism" theory never was a burning reality in anybody's life. In Bible times disciples continued to be baptized in the Spirit – in Samaria, Ephesus and Caesarea.

Baptism in the Holy Spirit is immersion in the Spirit. Considering that the Spirit is the operating power of God, it should be noticeable if we are immersed in him! It takes rare faith (or credulity) to believe one receives blessings which are never felt and leave no traceable result. But that is doctrine held by many, that when we first turn to Christ and Jesus saves us that is all, a comprehensive, once-and-for-all spiritual package. The problem was how or why

a 2nd Work of Grace is needed

this third person, **the** Third Person, came onto the scene later. But the fact of the matter is that that is what happens, and our theology has to fit the fact.

What then happens? Paul says that our bodies are the temples of the Holy Spirit. A Bible illustration is provided in the Bible account of the dedication of Solomon's temple. We are given full details. This wonderful temple stood for nothing else than a resting place for the Sinai stone tables of the Ten Commandments of the law. They had been placed in the Ark of Witness. That Ark rested in the inner chamber of the temple, the Holy of Holies. The tablets of the law made the Ark holy, and the Ark made the temple holy. The nearer things were to the Ark containing the Commandment tablets the more holy they were. The fact that they were in Jerusalem made it the holy city, Canaan the holy land.

> Baptism in the Holy Spirit is immersion in the Spirit.

The Ark itself had a top of solid gold called the mercy seat, and above it in solid gold were two winged cherubim. The glory of God (the *Shekinah*) appeared at the point between the cherubim. The Holy of Holies had no windows, candles, or lamps. It was lit by the glory of God.

When the temple was ready, King Solomon offered a dedicatory prayer. Then something happened: *"Fire came down from heaven [...] and the glory of the Lord filled the temple. The priests could not enter the temple of the Lord because the glory of the Lord filled it"* (2 Chronicle 7:1-2). That glory had previously been seen by nobody but the High Priest, and now the whole temple area was illuminated by it.

This was a pre-figuration of the day of Pentecost far ahead in time. On that day, 50 days after Christ had ascended to the Father, he sent fire from heaven. It appeared visibly on the disciples (Acts 2:3). From that day the glory of God and the Holy Spirit has rested on the whole church, the temple which is the body of Christ.

The Holy Spirit rests not only on the whole spiritual temple, but occupies the heart of every believer. We are the shrine of the Holy Spirit: *"If anyone does not have the Spirit of Christ, he does not belong to Christ"* (Romans 8:9). Then, as with the temple when the glory of God came forth from the Holy of Holies, when the baptism of the Spirit takes place, the Holy Spirit fills not only the shrine of the believer's heart but their whole being. We become physically as well as spiritually his dwelling, and as at Solomon's temple there is an outward manifestation showing that God has taken up his dwelling place. He makes his home with us (John 14:23).

Teaching about the baptism in the Spirit, however, does not rest on Bible types and shadows, or on a logical deduction from a series of texts, but by a clear promise given in the Word of God. It is not a metaphorical blessing but real. God does baptize in the Spirit. It is sound doctrine. This truth is not verbal reasoning, theologians thinking things out, but what God promised and does. He does guide us into all truth and by confirmation of his Word. Human speculation can no more anticipate God's mind than forecast what tune the wind whistles as it blows over the Rockies. True theology is a statement of what God does. Theology has no purpose at all unless it touches human need, God coming to us, saving, blessing, healing, seeking us as worshipers, and filling our lives with his glory.

Part 2

Holy Spirit baptism identifies Jesus. John the Baptist was sent to announce the Coming One, but nobody knew who John was talking about. He had to describe him, or the people would not be able to recognize him. He said, *"It is he who will baptize with the Holy Spirit"* (John 1:33). His distinguishing feature would be that he would baptize in the Spirit. It distinguishes nobody else. Jesus alone is the Baptizer in the Holy Spirit and fire. Nobody else can do it, give it, or impart it. It is God's own right and prerogative. The reason is that the baptism is not merely incoming power, but God himself, the Holy Spirit. Nobody can give God as if he were a commodity.

The baptizer in the Spirit – that is Jesus. If the Church preaches Christ at all, that is who he is, forever. A Jesus who does not baptize in the Holy Spirit and fire is not truly the Bible Jesus. Nobody has the right to preach Christ other than the Bible Christ who baptizes in the Holy Spirit and he is *"the same yesterday and today and forever"* (Hebrew 13:8). He is the God of faithfulness, always true to himself, to us and to his promise.

Something positive is happening to people today. It carries every Bible mark of what Jesus promised. It has no other explanation but that he is keeping his Word, baptizing in the Holy Spirit. There is no argument against it. It is happening.

However, preaching the Christ who baptizes in the Spirit can be academic, just repeating something that has been learned. The appropriate way is to preach what is experienced. Witnessing to

Christ was never intended to be verbal only. We ourselves are witnesses, evidence of Jesus, saying, "He saved **me**, baptized **me**, and
healed **me**! He is with **me**." The apostles who were dragged before the arrogant authorities bore the impression of the Holy Spirit.
Their unshakeable witness and confidence created astonishment.
The Spirit is not just a surge within believers' souls, but may show
in body language – personality, ways, voice, eyes, in the fruit of
the Spirit, attitudes people never suspect of themselves. Nothing is
more off-putting than the put-on pose of a Holy Joe.

Part 3

Easter

To understand the baptism in the
Spirit properly, our starting point is the
resurrection of Jesus. At first, the disciples did not believe he had risen; an
entombed corpse could not re-appear
and walk around talking to people. A
few women were adamant that they
had seen him, but to the men it did not
make sense. Women were not regarded
very highly in those days and Jesus
rebuked the disciples for sharing the
common view and not believing them.

> True theology
> is a statement of
> what God does.
> Theology has no
> purpose at all unless it
> touches human need,
> God coming to us,
> saving, blessing,
> healing, seeking us
> as worshipers,
> and filling our lives
> with his glory.

It has been said so often that the disciples became bold and jubilant
witnesses when they saw him risen from the dead. It is true, of
course, that unless Jesus had risen they would never have witnessed
at all. Nevertheless, at first they were unbelieving and anything

but jubilant. The rulers had arrested and executed Jesus and they could very well have decided to hunt his followers, too. The disciples hid, locking themselves in a room. Jesus actually did appear to them but even then some doubted the evidence of their own eyes. That is understandable. In the entire world's experience such a thing had never happened before. It contradicted all experience. For fear, the disciples hung back out of sight and kept quiet, for about six weeks according the Acts of the Apostles.

We know, of course, that the disciples did become bold and powerful witnesses. If it was not the knowledge that Christ had risen, what was it that brought about that change in them? Obviously, it had to be something! That something had already been promised by God, but it was not a "something" at all; it was a Someone, the Holy Spirit. He gave them assurance. He baptized them in fire, setting their knowledge of Christ ablaze.

This was why Jesus told them to wait before confronting the world with the gospel. They were not going out to lecture on the phenomenon of resurrection, trying to convince people that it happened, presenting cold facts. A claim of the dead rising was very controversial and people would dispute what they claimed. Listeners would argue, defend their disbelief, or even if they accepted what the disciples said, would push it aside as just another of the strange things that happen in our world, a bit of curious lore.

However, they were witnesses, not controversialists. No, they did not see him rise from the dead, but they had better evidence than visual. This message was vital, life-changing and life-giving. Presented casually, coolly, in a "believe it if you like" manner, it would do nothing. It had to be preached as a glorious and vital fact, by people with some kind of passion, not dispassionately, but by witnesses obviously electrified by what they announced, examples of what they preached – very much alive.

Jesus told them, *"Do not leave Jerusalem, but wait for the gift my Father promised, which you have heard me speak about. In a few days you will be baptized with the Holy Spirit. You will receive power when the Holy Spirit comes on you; and you will be my witnesses"* (Acts 1:4-5,8). Jesus made a great deal of that Someone, the Holy Spirit. He spoke of his coming and his work as absolutely essential and called him *"another Counselor,"* another like himself. Christ took the disciples by their lapels, so to speak, saying they must listen to what he had to say, that he was leaving them only so that Someone could come. That is the measure of the importance of the coming of the Holy Spirit.

What the Spirit of the Lord would do would be their making, turning them into torches. He would be – and still is – the key to effective witnessing. Jesus said, *"Apart from me you can do nothing"* (John 15:5); we have to remain in the vine, deriving life from him. The life of the Spirit is the secret of new disciples. We can do a great deal without the Holy Spirit, but nothing of any lasting effect.

Jesus said they would receive the Spirit in a few days. It happened just as he said, actually 50 days after the crucifixion, on the feast day of Pentecost (or Festival of Weeks). In the temple they were celebrating the barley harvest with a sheaf waved before God. This was the appointed day. Heaven touched earth and God the Holy Spirit from heaven began his operations here. At that point in time the Holy Spirit entered the world. The spiritual order became the age of the Holy Spirit. It was the inauguration of a new era.

> No word in the New Testament suggests that we do not need what the apostles had, or that what they had could be only for them.

On that Pentecostal day, they began *"to preach the gospel with the Holy Spirit sent from heaven"* (1 Peter 1:12). His was a positive descent and entrance into the world as much as when Jesus came from heaven. *"The Word became flesh"* (John1:14) – that was Jesus' entrance through the door of Bethlehem.

He clothed himself with human form and, similarly, the Holy Spirit garbed himself with the disciples as he took up residence with them. The world could not receive him, but hundreds loved Jesus and a group of 120 of them became the first Spirit-filled people on earth, men, women, apostles and disciples. They were simply sitting together, not standing, not kneeling or praying, just waiting as Jesus had instructed them: *"Do not leave Jerusalem, but wait for the gift my Father promised"* (Acts 1:4). Christ ascended to heaven and asked the Father to send his gift, the Holy Spirit, and within 10 days he had come.

That day was one of God's real diary dates. Like a tidal wave the Holy Spirit arrived and submerged the assembled company, the same infinite Person whose power shaped the furthermost edges of the universe. He filled them with himself, the living Spirit of God. Flesh and blood became his dwellings.

The Spirit did not come quietly. He announced his arrival through the 120. He gave utterance to it through the assembled believers in tongues and prophecy. For the disciples and apostles this was their greatest day.

The Holy Spirit is the love Spirit of Father and Son: *"God has poured out his love into our hearts by the Holy Spirit, whom he has given us"* (Romans 5:5). That love began to move the believers and operate through them. What they became was what the Spirit made them.

That event is the model. Believers who already trust Christ can know the Spirit in this further and more dynamic way. The apostles are our Christian models. Who else could be? Even in Biblical times, other people had the same experience: As Peter discovered, *"God gave them the same gift as he gave us, who believe in the Lord Jesus Christ"* (Acts 11:17). This baptism was for them as individuals, not "for the whole church." Others, like the household of Cornelius received the Spirit for themselves. No word in the New Testament suggests that we do not need what the apostles had, or that what they had could be only for them. On the contrary, Peter's message was clear: *"You will receive the gift of the Holy Spirit. The promise is for you and your children and for all who are far off – for all whom the Lord our God will call"* (Acts 2:38-39).

If the disciples needed to be so endued and to preach the gospel with the Holy Spirit and with manifestation of the Almighty, are we better than them, able to carry on God's work without the empowerment they had? We surely need everything that God can give us, and the world needs people equipped like that.

Part 4

For centuries people recognized the need for such a filling of God but tending to think it was not available today; only in recent times have people realized that is it the birthright of all believers. Today some half billion or more on earth know it and millions enjoy it.

The promise through John is a "baptism" of the Spirit and fire. The Greek word *baptizo*, now a religious expression, originally meant "to dip." John the Baptist "dipped" people in Jordan River. The word commonly referred to cloth being dipped in dye, the cloth in the dye and the dye in the cloth. It is a picture: the believer in the Spirit and the Spirit in the believer. Just as the cloth took on the character of what it was dipped into, believers take on the nature of the element into which they are baptized, which is likeness to God through the Holy Spirit.

It is startling to realize that Jesus actually left this world so that the Holy Spirit could come. *"Unless I go away, the Counselor will not come to you"* (John 16:7). His coming to us is mysterious but real.

Of course, many questions are asked when God is at work. People wonder if the baptism in the Spirit is a "second" blessing after being born again. Was the day of Pentecost baptism once and for all times? Were disciples baptized by proxy for the whole church for ever? One baptism, many fillings?

We will look at these kinds of questions again later in this book (in chapter 12, for example), but, however knowledgeable we are, we need to be aware that God's works are so often beyond our mental capacity to categorize and put them in convenient packages. Our inability to analyze or describe what happens does not make what God is doing any less true. God is above our rationalizing. The baptism in the Spirit is like the atonement, for which there are various theories; the fact of the matter is that Christ plunged to depths nobody will ever fathom. How the Father was reconciled to us by the death of his Son, whom we killed, is beyond the workings of the human mind. We know something took place that guarantees our salvation. Similarly, Jesus does baptize in the Holy Spirit, and we do receive power when the Holy Spirit comes upon us. It is his work and we are his agents. We can go with the Word knowing God never fails (see Acts 1:7).

> Just as the cloth took on the character of what it was dipped into, believers take on the nature of the element into which they are baptized, which is likeness to God through the Holy Spirit.

After the resurrection the disciples, shaken and scared, hiding away for fear of what might happen to them, certainly needed that baptism and to be endued with power – and so do we. And God will give us what we need: *"God will meet all our needs according to his glorious riches in Christ Jesus"* (Philippians 4:19). No change in the world makes the power of the Spirit unnecessary. We have no alternative to the power of the Spirit, no method, manner, scheme, or approach. The Spirit must do the work. The world still needs saving, still needs convincing, and it is impossible without the Holy Spirit.

The Holy Spirit is not a sense of awe floating around old religious property. If the Spirit is to be manifested it is through people, the Spirit-filled. The message to believers is: *"Be filled with the Spirit"* (Ephesians 5:18). We would not need to be told to be filled if we could live without being filled.

Jesus said we should ask, seek, and knock for God gives the Spirit to people who ask (Luke 11:9-13). That does not mean a casual moment of asking, but being open to God at all times – askers, seekers, knockers. God will acknowledge those who stand ready for the blessing. He has given us his Word, and we must grasp his promise.

> The first believers to receive the Holy Spirit are the original brand. They were what Christians are; to be what they were, we need the same Spirit.

"Be being filled": Preachers often explain that the Greek means "be being filled", but misunderstand it just the same. It certainly does not mean seek new fillings from time to time, but the very opposite. The verb in Greek indicates a continuing condition, a state of being filled. Once received, the Holy Spirit "abides" and does not evaporate, nor needs replenishment or renewing. It is a present ongoing state comparable to standing in a flowing river. In the Book of Acts good men were chosen because they were full of the Holy Spirit, their regular character.

To be filled we do what Jesus said – ask. That does not mean to make a leisurely request; asking, knocking, and seeking is

---

The Greek word *pleerousthe* from the root word *pleroo*, to fill, is a passive imperative in the present continuous.

a lifestyle. The Holy Spirit comes when he wants to those who are ready. We do not obtain the Holy Spirit like chocolate out of a machine, pull the lever and it is there. On the other hand, he does not mean us to ask for ever, always seeking but never finding. *"He who seeks finds"* (Luke 11:10) and they know when they have found what they sought. The baptism in the Holy Spirit is received by faith, but the evidence is signs following.

The apostles knew that the Italian people at Caesarea had received the Holy Spirit, because they heard them speak in tongues. That is the sure sign he wants us to have. Christianity demands faith but responds to faith – God is not our faith in God. The promise is *"like a peg in a firm place,"* to use Isaiah's expression (Isaiah 22:23). The first believers to receive the Holy Spirit are the original brand. They were what Christians are; to be what they were, we need the same Spirit.

Part 5

Do all who receive the Holy Spirit speak in tongues? The general answer is a firm, "'yes" – or would be, if everything in this world was perfect. God has no rules. What he does is what he can do, according to our faith. To say people can be baptized without tongues would not fit the New Testament very comfortably because

> The Spirit is not given at the will of man, but is a sovereign act of God.

every instance shows pretty surely that they all spoke in tongues. If people have absorbed fears about tongues, have had confused teaching, or for another – possibly subconscious – reason, the

Spirit can be quenched, preventing him from doing everything he normally would, that is to give signs. Some have faith for the Holy Spirit but not for tongues, so they are given in accordance with their faith. The crucial question for them is how do they know that they have been Spirit-filled without the evidence of being able to speak in tongues?

It is so vital that we **know** we are Spirit-baptized if we are to go out and face the challenge of the godless world. With that knowledge we can dare to go forth and know he is with us. The disciples had that assurance. Can we do without it? They knew the Spirit was with them and therefore: *"The disciples went out and preached everywhere, and the Lord worked with and confirmed his word by the signs that accompanied it"* (Mark 16:20). Holy Spirit ministry is attested by signs – if we believe.

It has been said that if anyone seeks the Spirit with the sign of tongues and does not receive the gift for a long time, they may feel disheartened, wondering if God is listening to them. Really? Should they then seek the Spirit without tongues? How will that help? What other way will they know that God is listening to them? Their "problem" over tongues is not solved by not believing in tongues.

Utterance in tongues does not come by trying. You don't "learn" how to speak in tongues. There is no technique, method, or even ministry. The Spirit is not given at the will of man, but is a sovereign act of God. This gift is not a talent, but God himself, the Spirit, not a power, or fire, but him. He is too awesome to be handled like plastic, dished out by glib over-sure arrogance. However, we can assist one another in prayer and by the laying on of hands as the apostles did in Samaria and Paul in Ephesus. Our attitude is to be humble and prepared. That is the lesson of Peter in the household of Cornelius – while he was still speaking, the Holy Spirit fell on them all.

In our crusade meetings, we always pray for everyone to be baptized in the Spirit. This was the command of God to us at the very beginning of our work. That Holy Spirit is now moving the nations. We are seeing the mightiest revival of all time. Millions who have been baptized in the Spirit with signs following go out confidently knowing that God will employ them as the instruments of his love and power. That is the power the 19th century believers believed in, the power that would equip them to evangelize the whole world.

*A miracle
is not the peak sign of God's presence,
nor is it the true purpose of seeking God.
Christianity is Christ.
We serve our Lord Jesus by the Holy Spirit.*

CHAPTER 5

"Times of refreshing shall come from the Lord."
Acts 3:19

God brings progress, initiating refreshing times. Advancement comes by sudden leaps, not at walking pace. The first major step forward came through Moses, 1,500 years before Christ; the world received the knowledge of the living God, a divine self-revelation of primary importance. It was not mere information, but saving knowledge. The next notable advance did not come for another 1,000 years, the upsurge in thought among the Greeks. The greatest advancement of all was Christianity. Many changes have followed, such as the Renaissance, the Reformation, the Industrial Revolution, and the scientific age, but the underlying change is the truth of Jesus Christ.

In the Christian age there have been Christian epochs. This book is about a new thing in Christian history, the Pentecostal/Charismatic and "renewal" movement, and the "re-discovery of the Holy Spirit." Millions of believers now have a new grasp of Bible promises. This world revival began on the first day of the 20th century in a remote corner (like the church in the "upper room" on the first day of Pentecost). It is all about a deepening of individual faith with great changes in worship styles and attitudes. It has affected almost all churches throughout the world. The Spirit-baptized can understand its heavenly impact.

19th century believers prayed for a worldwide revival – and were heard. The renewal movement is itself world "revival." The word "revival" is not a Bible expression but was chosen to describe a particular type of spiritual event. Christianity itself is revival.

> Being changeless, God's power has no degrees, no human "good, better, best." Everything he is, perfection and omnipotence, is behind everything he does.

People call some events "revival" and then ask what revival is! It is obviously only what we say it is, not something that God talks about.

Revival is often described as an "extraordinary work of God." That is a fair description from the human angle, but is it correct to think of God making a special exertion from time to time? Does it sit comfortably with what God says about himself, that he never changes? He does not do anything by half, but always with the full zest of his greatness. Just as the sun shines at the noon meridian, God is always at peak, with *"no shadow of turning,"* as James 1:17 (KJV) says, always fully himself, totally committed. Being changeless, God's power has no degrees, no human "good, better, best." Everything he is, perfection and omnipotence, is behind everything he does.

If 19th century believers, our great-grandparents, could see Christian life today, they would be struck by the Holy Spirit emphasis, Christian attitudes strongly Holy Spirit orientated. As a result Jesus is in clearer focus, personal, a friend in daily life. Spirit-anointed worship has brought new worship styles, new types of song as many as 90 years ago with such words as "Jesus! Jesus! Jesus! Sweetest name I know. Fills my every longing. Keeps me singing as I go!" [1]

---

[1] Written by Luther B. Bridgers in 1910.

Holy Spirit renewal has been called "Jesus religion." A blurred focus of the Holy Spirit blurs the view of Christ, for the Spirit alone reveals him.

Jesus said, *"When the Counselor comes, whom I will send to you from the Father, he will testify about me"* (John 15:26) and *"He will bring glory to me by taking from what is mine and making it known to you"* (John 16:14). The Christian faith is more than a supernatural faith. Manifestations are the outward mark. The greatest work God did or ever will do was to give his Son for our salvation. That tremendous operation should occupy our thoughts before anything else. It certainly concerns God before anything else. A miracle is not the peak sign of God's presence, nor is it the true purpose of seeking God. Christianity is Christ. We serve our Lord Jesus by the Holy Spirit.

> God works in this life through people only. A heart of faith, a mind to plan, and a hand to work always attract the power of the Holy Spirit.

The 120 disciples who were gathered together on the day of Pentecost received the Holy Spirit. We are not told what that did for them throughout the whole of their lives. The Bible is not big enough for that, but the general effect might be judged by the fact that they made their way at all in the dreadful world of 2,000 years ago. We are the their fruit, converts through Peter, James, John, Mary and her sisters in Christ, ordinary people made extraordinary by the Acts 2 experience, which is God's promise for us today.

If there is any disappointing to be felt, it is why this present-day Holy Spirit revival has come so late in the Church's story.

God is almighty but … he does what he can when he can, and cannot always do what he wants when he wants because that would be to do away with the free will that he gave us. Two initial elements are necessary, preaching and witness of the Word and prayer, as well as the response of hearers.

God works in this life through people only. A heart of faith, a mind to plan, and a hand to work always attract the power of the Holy Spirit. There can never be a void in the life of anyone of that caliber. God is short of such characters. If we want to serve the Lord, the Lord wants us to serve him, and has some service for us to perform. This is life's highest privilege and destiny.

CHAPTER 6

Holy Spirit Fire and Passion

"The silence of God" has been a popular theme, but it misrepresents God. Christ's name, "the Word," hardly suggests a silent God. On the day of Pentecost the Holy Spirit spoke through 120 throats. He came with the noise of a tornado, and inspired a roar of praise of 120 men and women speaking in tongues. They spoke, but he gave them utterance – a noise directly echoing God's noise. We read that it attracted an enormous crowd. God came out from the hiding places of his power and revealed himself. There was motion and commotion.

God is never dumb. David makes that point very strongly and mocks heathenism with its gods that have *"mouths but cannot speak"* (see Psalms 115:5). In 1 Corinthians, Paul also contrasts *"dumb idols"* (1 Corinthians 12:2) with the vocal gifts of the Spirit, tongues, prophecy, and interpretation, the word of knowledge, and the word of wisdom. These utterances are God's gifts, typical of God who speaks. They are wonderful, utterly beyond human invention. Nobody suggested them to God. These unique "gifts" express his nature. It would be hard to find a line of Scripture on which to build a doctrine of a silent God. It is not at all the Bible picture. People called on God because that is how they knew him – a God who can be heard. A silent heaven is frightening: *"If you remain silent, I will be like those who have gone down to the pit,"* the Psalmist cried (Psalm 28:1).

God speaks because he wants to speak, not because we urge him.
It arises from his character and disposition. He does not whisper.
At least, he did not whisper when he made known his will at Sinai.
His voice was like a trumpet and the mountain shook and vibrated.
The people begged Moses, *"Speak to us yourself and we will listen.
But do not have God to speak to us or we will die"* (Exodus 20:19).
One old hymn ran "Listen for the whispers of Jesus." The gospel
from which the hymn-writer drew that line is certainly not in my
Bible. We do not hear of Jesus speaking quietly, but we do hear of
him speaking very loudly, calming the sea, casting out foul spir-
its, raising Lazarus, preaching to massed thousands. Even on the
Cross in his last moment he gave up his spirit *"in a loud voice"*
(Matthew 27:50).

God is positive and hearty (to use a human description) and his
words are dynamic and throbbing. Anything associated with God
is alive. All nature, the globe burgeoning with a million orders of
life, is his work of art. The nature of God is love – love of an inten-
sity and ardent heat expressed throughout the glory of creation and
in the great passion of Christ on the Cross. The universe is God's
exclamation mark that was there when the Word spoke.

The Bible God is not served with subdued quietness. Speechless
silence and motionless stillness are not appropriate signs of the
Jesus who baptizes in the Holy Spirit and fire, and who reminded
his disciples of the words *"Zeal for your house has eaten me up"*
(John 2:17, NKJV). Worship as described for us in Scripture is
certainly not imbued with careful dignity. The word itself suggests passion, falling prostrate in adoration, in music, singing and
instrumentation, jubilation.

We would need to be surprised if the effect of that God of high passions coming on believers were to leave them silent. Speaking in tongues is the kind of thing we would expect. Never in Scripture do we find worshipers meeting together for silent meditation – Quaker or Buddhist style. In one early church meeting *"they raised their voices together in prayer to God"* (Acts 4:24). They are always vocal. Prayer was never silent. When one woman prayed silently, with only her lips moving, the High Priest of Israel thought she was drunk (1 Samuel 1:13-14). In Christian history silent prayer was unknown for centuries.

Given this massive testimony to fervor in worship and to the character of God, speaking in tongues hardly seems out of place!

There does seem to be an issue here. Human nature is not passionless. Modern civilization tames us, cages us, and forbids us to roar. It produces the urban man, mild, drab, and controlled: Mr. Smith on the 8.20 to town. The loss of true faith quells our temperament and dulls the sparkle. The man full of the Holy Spirit has a charismatic glow about him. We are made in God's image and he is not an unmovable, unemotional being – at least, not as the Bible depicts him. Alcohol, to be filled with spirits, is one way of removing the dullness, but to be filled with the Holy Spirit is a considerably better way.

> The loss of true faith quells our temperament and dulls the sparkle. The man full of the Holy Spirit has a charismatic glow about him.

The worship of God is the best of all opportunities as an outlet for exuberance. To worship God we should let our spirit soar without the weights and fears of social custom to repress us. Religion, of some sort, has always been the outlet for certain aspects of human nature. The worship of God lifts the spirit to its full emotional stature. Awe at God's greatness, devotion and adoration should allow us to be our own uninhibited selves, "naked before God," transformed.

In the Old Testament, there is little about true worship. David dancing half-naked through the streets in delight before God, much to the disgust of Michal his wife, was perhaps unusual. Nonetheless, the word "worship" does have physical overtones and it was not particularly unusual for people to prostrate themselves in worship.

> The nine-fold fruit of the Spirit does not include dignity. Dignity is no response to Christ crucified.

Preachers often quote football to Christians as an example of enthusiasm. The game is recognized as a traditional opportunity to explode. Other games are exciting, but spectators are more subdued. The atmosphere at a big match is part of the secret of football popularity. The stadium is almost sacred to it, like a shrine where supporters can let go without restraint and adulate their team. Nobody thinks it odd as everybody does the same. Why not? Such an occasion shows human nature undisguised.

There are enemies of passion. In the 19th century Schopenhauer condemned passion as blind, mindless striving while the postmodern attitude of detachment treats everything as a joke.[1]

---

[1] Nick Pollard, "Talking about sport" in IDEA (magazine of the Evangelical Alliance), July 2006.

The first law of all laws is to *"love the Lord your God with all your heart and with all your soul and with all your mind and with all your strength"* (Mark 12:30). That is a call to be totally passionate; the highest degree of exuberance would surely be appropriate, more than at any ball game. Mel Gibson's film *The Passion of the Christ* portrayed the inhuman cruelty inflicted on Jesus but there was one thing the film lacked: It could have made it clearer what Jesus was passionate about. It was his passion to do the will of God and to redeem the lost world. If football gets us going more than God, then we have our wires crossed somewhere.

It is one of the greatest tragedies in history that the church should have decided to adopt the attitude of subdued emotions for worship. Calling that solemnity "reverence" is an abuse of the English language. How "reverent" is it to be glum when remembering all God has done for us?

Our efforts **not** to be emotional when God is in view must come as a surprise to God. Is he happy with switched-off worshipers, deadpan faces, as rigid as gravestone figures? Would we ourselves want visitors who were like icebergs or Egyptian mummies? God, the fountain of life, needs lifeless representatives like we need a pain in the neck. Frigid worship is excused as "dignified." The nine-fold fruit of the Spirit does not include dignity. Dignity is no response to Christ crucified. In Scripture worshipers fall at the feet of Christ. On the day of Pentecost believers were thought to be drunk as they left the upper room. As far as I know, no one leaving Westminster Abbey or St. Peter's in Rome has ever been suspected of having had too much to drink!

How did the Church become so unreflective of what God is; why did it assume such an eccentric pose? God is a consuming fire! Christianity began with speaking in tongues but something along the way turned worship into a routine performance by priests watched by subdued congregations. Somehow faith and understanding in the power of the Spirit faded, becoming more and more corrupted until it was hardly more than a superstition.

If we look back to the years after the apostles, we find that the records for a couple of generations have been lost, destroyed in Roman persecutions. Then from about AD150 comes the account of Bishop Montanus and his followers. They prophesied and claimed the gifts of the Spirit. Their worship was fervent and free, a reaction against the cold and formal worship which prevailed at the time. The bishops condemned Montanism because prophesying could undermine their own authority, but also because it was so emotional. From that time on not only were spiritual gifts considered to be the domain of sacramental priests only, but fervor in religion was condemned as "enthusiasm," meaning that the people were "possessed." Warm worship was frowned on, the Spirit quenched, and passionless worship dominated. Formalism has marked church life for long centuries.

Human beings are not passionless by nature. Down the centuries there are frequent examples of passion breaking out of its religious straitjacket. Church history includes episodes of various kinds of vigorous religion, often too vigorous and warlike. The Catholic Church was not a solid changeless block but a mass of sects, cults, messiahs, break-away groups with a variety of ideas about God and worship. When expectations of Christ's return flared up, passions were rife. In one startling episode, for about 200 years hundreds of men and women, the Flagellants, walked through towns preparing for Christ covered in blood and lashing themselves, a medieval form of revival, but Flagellant types appear periodically, as they do even today in Mexico and the Philippines, for example. Extremists are always with us, but pushing them out of the door lets in creeping spiritual paralysis.

Nearer to our own times, in the 18th and 19th centuries, fervent faith did reappear. Wesleyan preaching often had a dramatic impact, with people responding with convulsions, noisy outcries and prostrations, and audiences gripped as if paralyzed, often seemingly swept with hysteria. Meetings where physical reactions took place came to be called "revivals" and usually characterized gospel meetings called "revival meetings" in the USA. Old-time revival effects occurred in Toronto a few years ago though no revival followed. It proved to be only the surf of the mighty ocean.

Of course, the question that arises when such scenes occur is always whether it all was of God. More Bible understanding of the Holy Spirit shows that the gospel should be in the power and demonstration of the Holy Spirit. Scripture does not detail what is meant by demonstration, but it is clearly some kind of visible or physical effect. God has granted us more knowledge of his promised power. Events of the Spirit are recognized according to the promise of the Word.

When Daniel and the Apostle John saw an angel, it prostrated them. Personality is a force. We react differently according to the kind of people we meet and the kind of people we are, stern or comical, gentle or brutal, but ultimately all personality comes from the Holy Spirit. Our own human presence is only a tiny spark of

his infinite presence. In him is everything we can imagine and
everything we are; anything anyone has ever been is only an atom
of his burning sun of wonder. If we watch a good comedian, we
generally smile (at least). If we see greatness, our response tends to
be one of admiration. If we see gentleness and kindness engraved
in a man or woman's features, we want to be like them.

We rejoice with them that rejoice and weep with them that weep.
We cannot help it. However, when the Spirit of the living God
falls on us, are we supposed to seize
up and freeze, becoming motionless
and unsmiling? On our way to church
we take in the glorious sunshine, the
majesty of the trees and splendor of the
green grass; it all puts a smile on our
face. But as soon as we reach the church
porch we switch our smile off. Is that a tradition to follow? If it is
an acceptable tradition for football fans to get excited at a match,
why should it be different at church? Why quench the Holy Spirit
and steel ourselves not to react to his manifest greatness? If God
had no effect upon our feelings, then we really ought to suspect
that spiritual death has taken place and *rigor mortis* set in.

> Living people
> respond to life.
> God is a living God,
> Jesus is the
> resurrection
> and the life

We recently carried out a small survey of people who had gone
down "in the Spirit" as they say. Everyone felt that their experience was supernatural and most people did not even know they
had fallen, at least for a few seconds. They felt at peace, enjoying
lying on the floor briefly. Overall, it left them with a powerful
sense of the presence of God. The work of the Spirit is always mysterious even though real. It has many outward signs, but the Bible

identifies speaking in tongues and prophecy as the norm for all believers, as assurance of the indwelling of the Spirit.

To outlaw emotion and physical display is unrealistic. God speaks of his own character of passionate love. If we want his Spirit, it is ridiculous to adopt an attitude at variance with his. Jesus showed considerable feeling, weeping, groaning, being moved with compassion in a manner that many of us in the West would find quite extreme. How then can suppressing our sensibilities in a stoical fashion, putting on a pose of self-congratulatory calm and self-possession attract the interest of a God whose very nature is love?

We can keep tight hold of ourselves, rein in and control our reactions, buttoning up our jacket and zipping up our composure. It may seem so strong and admirable, but where is the entrance or the welcome sign for the Holy Spirit? The promise was that *"a little child will lead them"* (Isaiah 11:6) – not a macho male. Leaning over the edge of the pulpit holding a friendly chat with the congregation, like a doctor advising a patient, has nothing in common with the driving force of the first Christians penetrating the pagan world. The present world needs the same kind of disciples.

Living beings are naturally equipped with emotions. When we have no feelings, we are dead. Until we are taken through the cemetery gates, some kind of emotion is always flowing across our consciousness. God who made us sends his Spirit upon us. Shakespeare used a wonderful picture: "Why should a man whose blood is warm within sit like his grandsire cut in alabaster?"[2] How can a pose of impassive silence be a recommendation for God? He

[2] William Shakespeare, *The Merchant of Venice*, Act 1, Scene 1.

is a God of fire, not an iceberg. Unless we show some signs of life who would suppose God is on us or among us?

Perhaps that is one reason why people keep clear of God – or the church, anyway. We can accuse them of unbelief and indifference, but could the cause be that "church" lacks signs of animation, and presents an image of frigidity and pedantic correctness? Living people respond to life. God is a living God, Jesus is the resurrection and the life, and is risen from the tomb, but those who represent him do not always reflect very much of resurrection life. It is fairly typical for religion to be regarded as the epitome of impassive rectitude. Not too much gusto please, keep everything under control, don't breathe – God is here! The dead have their ornate shrines in ancient churches, but there is no shrine for Jesus. Services where God seems to be in a coffin have nothing to do with the Risen Jesus. The Baptism of the Holy Spirit is a baptism of life, energy, zest. The Spirit-baptized are never comfortable in a cold church.

Healings, tongues, prostrations, outcries or other phenomena, the power of the Holy Spirit can be expected to have some impact upon our sensibilities. It seems perfectly sensible to anticipate excitement and wonder in his presence. Then, as he is Lord of heaven and earth, it is hard to see how the supernatural would not put in an appearance sooner or later.

Winning Millions to Christ

...One Soul at a Time

On target for 100 Million Souls in this decade!

For over thirty years, Christ for all Nations, the ministry of Evangelist Reinhard Bonnke, has been proclaiming the gospel of Jesus Christ across the continent of Africa and around the world. Since the year 2000, over 43 Million positive decisions have been recorded at his meetings.

احتفالات الإنجيل العظيم

(Left) The crowd rejoices as witchcraft fetishes and idols are burned and bondages are broken.

(Below) Every available space is taken at the morning *Fire Conference* where the dynamics of Holy Spirit Evangelism are taught.

Juba, Southern Sudan. 120,000 people in a single service hear the all-powerful message of salvation and together proclaim the name of Jesus!

Juba Sudan

Rivers of Blessing beside the River Nile.

After years of conflict in the war torn Southern Sudan, the Good News of Jesus Christ and His wonderful salvation is proclaimed.

Gospel Celebration احتفالات with Evangelist Reinhard Bonnke

The streets of Juba were empty as each night almost all of its inhabitants made their way to the crusade site to take part in this first ever Gospel celebration since the cessation of hostilities.

During 5 days of meetings over 580,000 people recorded decisions for Jesus Christ.

(Above) It seemed as if the whole of Ikom had poured out onto the streets to welcome the CfaN team and the arrival of the Evangelist.

(Below) Church leaders from Ikom and the neighboring country assembled at the local sports ground to be part of the *Fire Conference*.

Ikom NIGERIA

Souls Saved, Lives Changed, Bondages Broken!

After being born blind, eight year-old Wilfred easily reaches up to snatch Bonnke's white handkerchief to demonstrate his ability to see.

(Right) Tens of thousands of prayer requests from the crowd and partners around the world are prayed for by all in attendance.

GREAT GOSPEL CAMPAIGN with REINHARD BONNKE

Changing lives, restoring families, touching communities... The Gospel message brings hope wherever it is proclaimed.

OGOJA

With a passion that has consumed his heart for over 35 years, Reinhard Bonnke preaches the message of Jesus Christ across the continent of Africa and around the world.

At every campaign, personal ministries are transformed and enfired to evangelism. Daily seminars empower and challenge. *Fire Conferences* raise up and multiply.

(Above) Healed during a previous crusade, this man testified to his healing from madness by showing scars that chains had once made on his wrist and ankles. Others gave thanks as they gave testimony of their healing.

The closing service at the Wukari *Great Gospel Crusade* was attended by over 200,000 pe

Wukari WELCOMES the GOSPEL!

The city center and surrounding areas celebrated the arrival of the signs-following Gospel message. It was a week of meetings characterized by the miraculous that would galvanize the Church to Soul-Winning.

Signs and wonders follow the preaching of the Word. Many come forward to testify of their healing while the crowd rejoices with dancing and singing.

During 5 days of meetings in Abuja, the capital city of Nigeria, over 1,040,000 souls record a positive decision for Christ.

Abuja, Nigeria

On Kingdom Business, at the Seat of Authority.

Empowered to Holy Spirit Evangelism, nearly 100,000 delegates attend the Fire Conference.

(Above) To the great joy of the gathered crowds, this young man demonstrates his ability to hear while another (left), his healing from blindness. At every crusade, there is prayer for the sick and a time when those whose lives have been touched can come forward to testify. (Opposite) Healed from deafness, this man demonstrates an ability to hear.

(Left) Each night multitudes respond to the Gospel call, are counselled, receive a 'Now that you are Saved' follow up booklet and are then directed to a local church.

UROMI

Light out of Darkness and Freedom for the Oppressed!

The Saturday evening meeting saw over 140,000 people witness an unprecedented surrender and burning of witchcraft items. Curses were broken, the sick were healed and the oppressed set free!

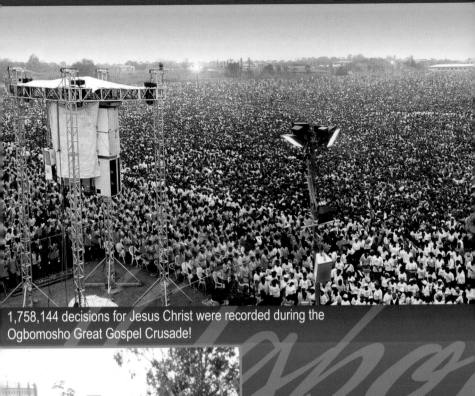

1,758,144 decisions for Jesus Christ were recorded during the Ogbomosho Great Gospel Crusade!

(Above) A full one hour before Evangelist Bonnke and his team arrived, the crusade ground overflows with souls hungry to hear the life-changing Gospel message.

Each night, the city's streets became a moving celebration as the people joyously make their way to the crusade site.

Ogbomosho

Multitudes, Multitudes in the Valley of Decision!

Tens of thousands of church workers and leaders receive a copy of *Evangelism by Fire*, a book written by Evangelist Bonnke to inspire all to Holy Spirit Evangelism.

FIRE CONFERENCES

Throughout the world, *Fire Conferences* are held for church leaders and evangelists. *"We must preach the Gospel in the power of the Spirit. It is the same Spirit of the prophets poured out upon all flesh today!"*

More than 95,000 leaders and workers form part of the crowd that attended the Abuja Fire Conference in Nigeria.

CHAPTER 7

The Story of the Holy Spirit Movement

Jesus, soon to ascend to God, was with his disciples. They asked him, *"Lord, are you at this time going to restore the kingdom to Israel?"* (Acts 1:6). They were on completely the wrong wavelength. Jesus told them that times and dates were not their concern; their business was to be witnesses. They wanted political independence for Israel, but he told them to look for the promised Holy Spirit. They still thought of Jesus as a possible political leader, a second Moses. Jesus had wider ideas than Israel. He told them to go to the ends of the earth with the gospel (Acts 1:8).

What has lately become known of the Holy Spirit – especially by experience – has leaped all barriers, linked believers of all names and varieties around the globe, and produced a new evangelistic keenness.

In 1999 Russell P. Spittler, Professor of New Testament, Fuller Seminary, wrote [1], "For the most part, they (the Spirit-baptized) don't know their own strength. In the last five percent of Christian history, they have become a major global force in Christendom – second only to the billion Catholics in the world and numbering about half the world's Catholics." It is a renewing force, mocking the wishful thinking of those who tell us gleefully that Christianity is declining.

[1] Pentecostal Currents in American Protestantism ©1999 University of Illinois press

A Bible College leader, Charles Parham, hit the target question. Going away and leaving some Bible work for the students, he suggested off the cuff that they search the New Testament for references to the sign of the Baptism in the Spirit. It was crucial. What they found was positive and unconfused. The empowering Holy Spirit signified his coming with speaking in tongues. On 1 January 1901, the first day of the 20th century, one of the young women members of Bethel Bible School in Kansas, Agnes Ozman, asked her fellow students to lay hands on her. She was filled with the Spirit and spoke in tongues.

Tongues were not new. Many had spoken in tongues. Now, however, they knew what it signified. Agnes knew. Here was the long-sought baptism in the Spirit, the promise of God for the resident Holy Spirit. Agnes died in 1937, but she lived to see what she had quietly received beginning to touch the nations. At that college in Topeka, after Agnes, a dozen others received the Spirit. The newly baptized students, full of the assurance of the Spirit, conducted missions here and there with powerful effect.

"Tongues"? A physical effect! To the sober Christian world it sounded extreme. Christians were unsure and shy. The baptism in the Spirit quickly brought opposition which spawned rumors of extravagance which became legends. Any stick will do to beat a dog.

Six years later in an old wood-framed Methodist church, a small group of seekers, black and white, met together; they understood the promise of the Word. Led by a black man, William Seymour, who indulged in no noisy spiritual performances but knelt quietly behind his old box lectern, he let the Spirit of God hold sway.

Then the howling hounds of the world press discovered what was going on. For them it was sensational and eminently reportable. The Christian world read, and became aware. Evangelicals had long prayed for "revival," that is Christian meetings with physical effects. Azusa Street in Los Angeles, California, drew believers from as far as Europe – all eager to know more. Nonetheless, their claims that their experience was actually Biblical and not a mere side effect of revival excitement, attracted criticism. For 50 years the churches treated tongues with suspicion, but in the 1960-70s Christian approval began.

The Holy Spirit began to reveal himself across the denominations. Soon, in many places a new liberty took the place of church traditions. Today the Holy Spirit has come into his own. A reviewer in the scholarly Expository Times stated that by the year 2000 there were about 500 million such charismatic people. By 2006 the figure is quoted as 600 million, a spiritual Big Bang flinging into the Christian firmament hundreds of thousands of new churches, organizations, charities, missions, colleges, scholars and millions of out-and-out Christians testifying to being "born again." What detonated it? Its divine qualities show us its origin.

> What has lately become known of the Holy Spirit – especially by experience – has leaped all barriers, linked believers of all names and varieties around the globe, and produced a new evangelistic keenness.

This world revival looks remarkably like what 19th century believers prayed for: "another Pentecost." The first disciples received power but never returned to the Upper Room for "another Pentecost." We do not read they had prayer retreats to recover

> The first disciples received power but never returned to the Upper Room for "another Pentecost." We do not read they had prayer retreats to recover power.

power. Once they had received the Holy Spirit they did not ask again for the Spirit. No "prevailing in prayer" to make sure God was with them. They knew he was!

Christianity itself is known properly only by experience, so is the Holy Spirit. It needs more than a book – this book, for example – but this book is written to bring the Holy Spirit experience to readers and to guide them in his ways and will.

CHAPTER 8

ก *Panachate*

The Paraclete

Jesus led the disciples to Mount Olivet and, from there, "ascended," went back to heaven. Then *"they returned to Jerusalem with great joy. And they stayed continually at the temple, praising God"* (Luke 24:52-53). Jesus left the disciples and they rejoiced! Joy at losing their Lord is not quite what we would expect. Never before or since has the loss of a loved one created joy. Only the "loss" of this One was something that could engender joy. There was something special about this event, some secret so wonderful that the disciples could not stop rejoicing. Parting from their dear friend was bound to cause their heart to ache, but clearly they knew that this was a small price to pay for the vast benefit that was going to follow.

Jesus had forewarned them that it would be like that: *"In a little while you will see me no more. You will weep and mourn while the world rejoices. You will grieve, but your grief will turn to joy and no one will take away your joy. A woman giving birth to a child has pain but when her baby is born she forgets the anguish"* (John 16:19-22).

Not too many seem glad today because Jesus has ascended to heaven. Who is happy about it? Most of the world would welcome him back. Yet if we knew what the disciples knew, we would have every reason to rejoice – some of us anyway. They had an understanding of which "the wise of this world" had not the slightest notion.

Well – don't we know? This chapter hopes to reveal the secret, an open secret which should create the same joy.

Liberal critics ridicule the Bible account of the Ascension as if they themselves were far superior to gospel writers. They mock the Ascension story with references to jet propulsion, blast off and a three deck universe. Such scorn does them no credit. Do modern critics really think that the Bible writers were so ignorant and naïve? Is that intelligent? It reveals the blindness of unbelief. The Ascension is part of a vast Bible canvas portraying Christ's coming from the Father and returning to him. Jesus did "ascend." How would critics describe it?

In fact, the church itself has not produced much great teaching on the Ascension. Usually it is referred to as his final triumph, the end of Christ's work. We sing, "All his work is ended, joyfully we sing, Jesus has ascended, glory to our king."[1] But his work did not end then at all, and never will. He went away to do something all-important.

The Lord's Ascension was an all-important appointment with the Father concerning the coming of the Holy Spirit, the Paraclete – bringing about a fundamental change in God's world order.

The first thing ever said about Jesus when he began his earthly work was by John the Baptist, his forerunner. John said the Coming

---

[1] From the hymn "Golden harps are sounding", words by Frances R. Havergal, 1871.

One would baptize with the Holy Spirit and fire (Matthew 3:11). The truth is, however, that up to the time when Jesus actually left the earth he had baptized no one with the Holy Spirit or with fire. Even John the Baptist was puzzled, and wondered if he had identified Jesus wrongly.

In fact, Scripture notes that when Jesus left earth the Holy Spirit was not here in that sense at all: *"Up to that time the Spirit had not been given"* (John 7:39). To be the Christ whom John identified, he had to baptize in the Spirit and Jesus did not ... then. John did not realize that his own prophecy indicated a far, far bigger work of the Baptizer in the Spirit than in the local and immediate sense.

The Ascension was necessary so that the Holy Spirit could be sent. Knowing the wonders Jesus performed, it might seem that he could have baptized anyone with holy fire. He did give the apostles power over evil and sickness (Matthew 10:1) but did not fill them with the Holy Spirit. The Holy Spirit had used certain individuals, such as Moses and the prophets, but Scripture never uses the language of people being "filled" with the Spirit until Jesus had ascended.

The Ascension was a tremendous divine drama affecting heaven itself and the whole future history of the world. It is an awesome concept, one difficult for our brain to register. In view is the Godhead entire. The Son of God, now the Son of Man, joined the Father and Spirit to send the Spirit into the world. The decision touched the heart of God's very being. That is the tremendous background to the baptism in the Spirit. Just as the Son had come and lived on earth, the Spirit should now come, take his place as the "Other Counselor," and make his home with us.

That happened. The Spirit did come and he is here now. The Holy Spirit is the creator of all things but, at the express wish of Christ, devoted himself to the problem of us, discreditable people. It was not a casual, easy arrangement. God holds the universe together. We may find it difficult to imagine a place where he is, but the divine counsel took place there; it is the power centre, and out of that centre the Spirit came to us.

That profound event took place because Christ loved us. The Spirit was his gift and the fulfillment of the Father's promise. Before the day of Pentecost, the Holy Spirit worked through Jesus doing the Father's will. The compassion of Christ mirrored the compassion of the Father. Jesus did what he saw was God's will and he never saw God not want to save, heal, or deliver someone coming to him. The love of God was the love of Father, Son and Holy Spirit.

> The Lord's Ascension was an all-important appointment with the Father concerning the coming of the Holy Spirit, the Paraclete – bringing about a fundamental change in God's world order.

The purpose of Christ's ascension was to rise to the centre of creation, the ultimate height of all existence, to the place of all power and authority, and to touch the heart and hand of omnipotence. Father, Son and Spirit conferred together, and by their will the Holy Spirit came, the love gift of the whole Godhead. That is the greatness of the Baptism in the Spirit. The Baptism in the Holy Spirit is not a wave-of-the-hand blessing. It is more than any blessing; it is God himself coming to us.

Around AD 45 someone carried a letter in their pocket to the Roman colony at Corinth. Written by Paul, it stood as a decree liberating the world from the confusion and oppression of pagan darkness. It read, *"Do you not know that your body is a temple of the Holy Spirit, who is in you, whom you have received from God?"* (1 Corinthians 6:19). Until then, God was a vague conception, indescribable and unreachable, absolutely perfect and too pure to have anything to do with gross flesh and vile bodies. Paul's revelation shattered Greek "wisdom." He let the light in for all to see the true and living God, warm, loving, his arms stretched towards us for us to experience him, his greatness permeating the consciousness and lives of ordinary mortals.

The Holy Spirit is the life of all God does. Christian experience comes by him. The work of Christ to be applied to our need is applied by the Holy Spirit, who applies it. Jesus did everything for us and everything he did was for us. He did nothing for himself or his own advantage. He came for us, was born for us, lived for us, ministered for us, taught and healed for us, suffered, died, rose and ascended for us, appears in the presence of God for us, and is coming back for us. He made us heirs to *"every spiritual blessing in the heavenly places in Christ"* (Ephesians 1:3 NKJV) – salvation, redemption, forgiveness, peace, power, gifts. The Spirit opens the treasury of all God's joys for us all.

> Just as the Son had come and lived on earth, the Spirit should now come, take his place as the "Other Counselor," and make his home with us.

The book of Hebrews paints the picture of Jesus having entered heaven's holiest place as our great high priest (Hebrew 4:14). It is a truth expressed more in our hymns than in pulpit ministry. Perhaps Christ's ascension, his going on high and leaving us, has not been proclaimed with great joy as being relevant to our lives down here. Popularly, it has been thought of as the end of his work on earth; he would now be eternally with his Father.

The truth is that his work has not ended. He had a particularly real work to do by rising to the Father. He said, *"Unless I go away, the Counselor [Paraclete] will not come to you"* (John 16:7). The Holy Spirit comes sent by the Father at the request of the Son – we have nothing to do with it. It is not our scheme. We would never think up such a thing. The Paraclete is always sent or comes because he wants to. It is his sovereign grace. He does what he does because he is who he is. We need him and he responds. We ask and we shall receive.

The name Paraclete – *Parakletos* in Greek – is found five times in the New Testament. English has no single equivalent word. It is translated by names like Comforter, Counselor, Advocate, and Lawyer. Looking at it in other Scriptures helps to show how Jesus used the term. "Parakletos" (related to the word *paraklesis* used 29 times in Scripture). It shows the Holy Spirit to be a counselor, assistant, advocate, helper, intercessor, advisor, someone called alongside to support us.

That is not all. The New Testament talks a great deal about the Holy Spirit, describing him. The Bible has a great interest in the Paraclete though the church has generally had such sketchy notions about him, making him almost a spare member of the Godhead called in only on special occasions.

Jesus has a special description of him: *"I will ask the Father, and he will give you another Comforter to be with you for ever – the Spirit of truth"* (John 14:16). "Another" means another beside Jesus. Jesus left them, but another One came to them. What they were empowered to do when Jesus was with them, they would do when this "another" was with them. Jesus was planning to go away, but he said, *"I will not leave you as orphans"* (John 14:18) (Greek *orphanos*, comfortless or bereft).

God planned it long before. Well in advance of the event, Jesus told the disciples, *"As long as it is day, we must do the work of him who sent me. Night is coming, when no one can work. While I am in the world, I am the light of the world"* (John 9:4). This predicted the three days when it would be night as he lay in the grave and could not perform the works of God. In fact, miracle healings did not occur until after seven weeks later, when he sent the Holy Spirit. Jesus told the disciples what it was going to be like: *"You will weep and mourn while the world rejoices. You will grieve, but your grief will turn into joy. Now is your time of grief, but I will see you again and you will rejoice"* (John 16:20-22). He rose from the grave and the light shone again. He demonstrated that he was the same Jesus. At the beginning of his work he had brought the disciples a miracle shoal of fish, and then after his resurrection he repeated the miracle but in greater style (John 21:6; Luke 5:6).

> The Holy Spirit comes sent by the Father at the request of the Son – we have nothing to do with it. It is not our scheme.

The disciples were disorganized and tottering until "another Comforter" came. The first words of Acts are: *"In the former book I wrote about all that Jesus began to do and to teach until the day he was taken up to heaven"* (Acts 1:1-2) (began – Greek *archomai*). Obviously, what he had begun was to be continued. Jesus said his works were to cease when it was night – when he lay in the grave – but after he rose, they would continue. Then he would work with the hands of the church, not with his own fleshly hands. What Jesus would do then was to be by the Holy Spirit – the same Spirit that would be given to those who believed, *"another parakletos"* beside himself. They would again go out on mercy miracle missions, as when Jesus was with them. Those missions had been part of his training for when the Spirit would come (Matthew 10:5; Luke 9:2).

The extraordinary thing is that Jesus said that because he was going to the Father, his disciples would not only do what he had done, but do greater works. Nobody ever has done greater miracles than Christ in the physical order.

What, then, has anybody done that is greater than anything Jesus did? His miracles of healing and his nature miracles are unequalled and bore the signs of absolute omnipotence. Yet he promised greater things.

What Jesus did was by the Holy Spirit: *"The one whom God has sent speaks the words of God, for God gives the Spirit without limit"* (John 3:34). Until he ascended to heaven, the Holy Spirit was not yet with us, only with Christ (John 7:39). Without the Spirit no one can do anything to bring power to bear against the world. However, Jesus said that when the Counselor (the Paraclete) comes, he will *"convict the world of guilt in regard to sin and righteousness and judgment"* (John 16:8). These things had never happened, not even when Jesus was preaching. It happened after the Holy Spirit burst in upon the first disciples. Endued with power from on high, Peter made 3,000 converts, men convicted of sin.

That is what the age of the Spirit was to be, the day of the Paraclete, sent as our abiding and all-powerful friend whose power is "toward" us, his resources ours. The Holy Spirit is not additional help. He is the heart and miracle of Christianity.

> The Holy Spirit is not additional help. He is the heart and miracle of Christianity.

The Paraclete

is always sent or comes

because he wants to.

It is his sovereign grace.

He does what he does because he is who he is.

We need him and he responds.

We ask and we shall receive.

CHAPTER 9

The Christ of the Spirit

Drew he was not God

If Jesus was God, why was he anointed with the Spirit? He was the Word made flesh. Wasn't that everything? Did he really need to be anointed? There is something really extraordinary about this!

Jesus lived in obscurity for 30 years and passed through all stages in a man's life. He lived a life of unparalleled perfection, to which God testified saying from heaven, *"You are my son, whom I love; with you I am well pleased"* (Mark 1:11). With such a divine endorsement, did Jesus need the Holy Spirit? Whatever we might think, in that first hour of introduction to the public arena the fact is that *"as soon as Jesus was baptized, he went up out of the water. At that moment heaven was opened, and he saw the Spirit of God descending like a dove and lighting on him"* (Matthew 3:16). John's Gospel points out that God gives the Holy Spirit *"without limit"* (John 3:34).

Acts 10:38 tells us that *"God anointed Jesus of Nazareth with the Holy Spirit and power and he went around doing good and healing all who were under the power of the devil, because God was with him."* Jesus applied a prophecy of Isaiah to himself: *"The Spirit of the Lord is on me, because he has anointed me to preach good news"* (Luke 4:18; Isaiah 61:1). The way John the Baptist knew that he would be able to identify Christ was that he would be the one to *"baptize you with the Holy Spirit and with fire"* (Matthew 3:11). The hallmark of the Christ was that he was the One with the Holy Spirit who would baptize us with the Spirit.

Jesus lived the life of a human person but a life that has been the greatest and most wonderful inspiration ever since. It is common to hear people say they would like to be like Jesus, to model their lives on his, to copy his character and selfless sacrifice. So it should be. But if we want to be like him, there is one all-important consideration that we cannot overlook. Jesus was filled with the Holy Spirit. For him to be our example we cannot omit the one great feature which made him what he was, the Holy Spirit. His very title, the *"anointed One"* says it all. It is what the word "Messiah" means. That is Jesus: the Word, the Anointed.

> Jesus showed us how he lived as the Son of Man so that we would know how to live as the children of God.

Luke's Gospel places considerable emphasis on the Holy Spirit – particularly in relation to Christ. First *"the Holy Spirit descended on him in bodily form like a dove"* (Luke 3:21), then *"Jesus, full of the Holy Spirit, returned from the Jordan and was led by the Spirit in the desert"* (Luke 4:1), and then *"Jesus returned to Galilee in the power of the Spirit"* (Luke 4:14). Then he quoted Isaiah, *"The Spirit of the Lord is on me"* (Luke 4:18) and added, *"Today this scripture is fulfilled in your hearing"* (Luke 4:21).

Without the Holy Spirit nobody can be what Jesus was **with** the Spirit, especially as he was the Son of God and we are only human. If he is our example and we must be like him, then we must also receive the Spirit of God. Many like to talk about following Jesus, stepping where He stepped but they fail before they start as they are not filled with the Spirit as he was. Jesus lived by the Spirit. He was the Christ of the Spirit. There is no other Christ. His experience as a man needed the Holy Spirit, and that should be our experience, too.

Jesus not only gave his life for us; he was also born and lived for us, demonstrating how to be what we should be. Jesus enacted in himself the whole of human life, birth, growth, and work, and an essential element was the indwelling Spirit. This is a pattern for the life of every Christian. We might consider the life of Jesus and despair, feeling that we could never even faintly reflect the divine glory of such a life. But that was not the idea at all. Looking at him was meant to give us hope, not fill us with guilt. God was with him and God is to be with us and that is by far the all-important thing. Jesus showed us how he lived as the Son of Man so that we would know how to live as the children of God.

The glorious truth of the presence of the Holy Spirit is one of the greatest joys of the Christian life. It is difficult to understand why the early church seems within a generation to have lost what we understand as the Scriptural Charismatic teaching and experience, so clearly laid down in the Word. That is judging from our limited understanding of those times and also by the legacy of the first fathers of the first-century church, at least from what we know of those early times. True enough, they did speak about the Holy Spirit in Christ, but mainly to point out that he existed as part of the Godhead; they had little to say about the experience of the Spirit. Ignatius of Antioch, who was martyred in AD 107, referred to the Holy Spirit and was a disciple of the apostle John, but he could hardly be called a Charismatic. The same thing can be said

200 years later in the writings of Basil the Great of Caesarea, born
in AD 329. These and others recognized the Holy Spirit in Christ
and that he was directed by the Spirit, but in an academic sense
and little more.

One of the great names soon after the apostles was Polycarp, who
was martyred about AD 160 by fire and sword. His famous words
are part of the golden treasury of Christian nobility. As an old
man, Polycarp chose to die rather than
deny his God, saying, "For 86 years I
have been his servant, and he has done
me no wrong. How can I blaspheme
the King who saved me?" We have a
letter he wrote about 70 years after the
apostles and he does not mention the Holy Spirit even once. What
makes this more surprising is that his friend was Ignatius, the disciple of John the Apostle.

> The church wants
> no dead limbs,
> no feet going to sleep,
> but everyone alive with
> the life of the Spirit.

In fact, not only was the Holy Spirit absent from this famous letter
of a famous Christian but Polycarp's idea of salvation also seems to
have slipped away from the grace of God to depend more on good
works. This was the laborious shape of the faith for a long time,
and it was the legacy of those very remote first years. During the
Roman persecutions martyrdom came to be regarded as the sure
way to heaven, rendering some so ready to die for Christ that a
Roman judge wondered how wretched these Christians must be
if they were so ready for death! For long centuries when Bibles
were rare and rarely opened, sincere men and women have tried
to attract God's favor and support by self-denial, prayer, fasting,
penitence, and creditable works. They were trying to be holy by
works not by grace.

After a brief episode when the followers of Montanus became known for fervent Holy Spirit worship, they were written off as heretics, and as a sect they were eliminated in AD 220. Nearly two millennia passed before the great truth of a Pentecost was realized for every believer. A day like Acts 2:4 was not only for the apostles but, as Peter announced, it was *"for all who are far off – for all whom the Lord our God will call"* (Acts 2:39). Holy Spirit truth became clouded over with other questions and teachings. But the Spirit is what we need in our weakness and imperfection to make our witness effective.

The God-Man

The church believed that Christ was God – a glorious and wonderful truth. His incarnation and Deity dominated church teaching for centuries. His wonders were seen as marks of his Godhead and as the manifestation of his own inherent divine power. He turned water into wine and *"manifested his glory"* (John 2:11); he healed many who were ill and demon possessed. His grace reduced a prostitute to penitential tears. These wonders are celebrated today as events of the days when God walked the earth in human form. We know that it was God incarnate who performed such deeds. That is a fundamental truth. The One who came and loved us was the Lord from heaven. The arms he put around the shoulders of weary men and weeping women were the mighty arms of God. These things bring joy to us today, and always will.

However, Jesus' works were evidence of another element beside his own Deity. He was anointed to perform such deeds, the God-Man filled with the Holy Spirit. He lived as we live, walking about and working, but something happened to him – the first time it had

ever happened to anyone. He became the first Man of the Holy
Spirit and performed mighty deeds not only as God, but by his
anointing (Luke 4). Being what he was and acting by his sovereign
will, he was "partnered" by the Holy Spirit. He did nothing on
his own. Jesus was the Man of the Spirit and the instrument of the
Father's will. Every miracle was a Godhead miracle.

which seem to be new

The Bible <u>portrait of Christ is not of</u> a god descending to earth
and doing the <u>impossible for</u> a short time, <u>scattering gifts</u> here and
there. From the beginning Jesus was one with the Spirit of God.
At the Annunciation, the archangel Gabriel said, *"The Holy Spirit
will come upon you and the power of the Most High will overshad-
ow you. So the holy one to be born will be called the Son of God"*
(Luke 1:35). Jesus was of the Holy Spirit from birth and all his
life was of the Spirit. When he appeared to begin his work as the

> It is the Holy Spirit
> that makes the body,
> bringing together
> its living elements.
> The church is God's
> dynamic force on earth.

Christ, the Spirit visibly came to him
and visibly associated with him. To
John the Baptist, what distinguished
Jesus from others was his Holy Spirit
character, the One to whom God gave
the Spirit and who baptizes in the Holy
Spirit out of his fullness.

Today we have grasped some fundamental encouragement. To see
the Holy Spirit, we look at Jesus. Jesus is the Revealer. He told
his disciples, *"If you really knew me, you would know my Father
as well"* (John 14:7). For the believers the Holy Spirit had not yet
come but Jesus ushered in the Kingdom and Kingdom power, the
power to be given to all who ask. Jesus had Holy Spirit fullness.

Jesus did not work as God on his own, independently. The Godhead never does that. It is wonderful to think that whatever God does for us, saving, healing, guiding, blessing, it is the heart-wish of Father, Son and Holy Spirit. The whole Trinity, the Godhead is behind it. However, what is done carries the distinctive mark of every member of the Godhead at work.

One question has been around for a long time – did Jesus heal people by gifts of the Spirit or by his own Deity? Neither alternative is correct. Jesus said, *"I do nothing on my own but speak just what the Father has taught me. The one who sent me is with me; he has not left me alone, for I always do what pleases him"* (John 8:28-29). What Jesus did was by the Holy Spirit not by his Deity operating in isolation; he is no soloist. Jesus healed a blind man and called it *"the work of God"* (John 9:3). No member of the Trinity ever acts independently. All miracles in this world are evidence of the hand of the Holy Spirit. Jesus, God in the flesh, was still dependent on the Father and the Spirit.

The Holy Spirit is called the *"Spirit of Christ"* (1 Peter 1:11), meaning that he is the Spirit who moved with and in Christ. The Spirit and Christ belong to one another together. The Gospels give us the divine portrait of Jesus, truly him. When we look at him, we also see the Holy Spirit. He was the instrument of the Spirit and the Spirit was the instrument of the Father.

This picture of the Christ of the Spirit, the Spirit directing him (Luke 4:1) represents God's ideal for all who love him. It also depicts God's plan for the church, *"the church which is his body"* (Ephesians 1:22-23). What Christ was in bodily form the Church is now. Christ's devotion to the will of God and his living action by the Spirit is the New Testament ideal for the church. It is true that the Holy Spirit acts when we act, and that works well when we are led by the Spirit. Without the Spirit our efforts fall flat. We must discern between egotism, arrogance, presumption, and dependent faith in God. Even Jesus, God in the flesh, insisted that he did nothing on his own, but that what he did was the work of the Father.

The Spirit-filled Church, representing the Spirit-filled Jesus

The picture of the church in 1 Corinthians 12 is quite startling. We are shown not only the intended unity of the church but also the place of the Holy Spirit in its work and in its very existence. Paul describes the body as made up of many members, but *"to each one the manifestation of the Spirit is given for the common good"* (1 Corinthians 12:7). Each one – not just the pastor or elders – everyone. No believer is on a higher spiritual level than another. The pastor "class" is not an indication of spiritual superiority. With God there is no distinction between priest and laity, for the Holy Spirit is with each person. He may operate though in a multitude of different ways though we all have the same anointing, if we are anointed at all. *"For we were all baptized by one Spirit into one body and we were all given the one Spirit to drink"* (1 Corinthians 12:13).

> The Holy Spirit awaits the Word and will show himself whenever the Word is proclaimed.

The church wants no dead limbs, no feet going to sleep, but everyone alive with the life of the Spirit. It is the Holy Spirit that makes the body, bringing together its living elements; what is needed is for the whole body to work together and move together in the same direction. The church is God's dynamic force on earth. We are told about *"the unity of the Spirit."* We are responsible for preserving the unity but the Holy Spirit is the unifying element. He holds us together – if we want to be together.

The "gifts" of the Spirit, some of which are named in this twelfth chapter of Paul's first letter to the Corinthians, are not exclusive awards for the special members; they are placed in the church because the church needs them. Paul likes lists. In Ephesians 4:11 he names some of the members needed in the Church: *"apostles, prophets, evangelists, pastors, and teachers."* However, others are needed and Paul extends his list in 1 Corinthians 12:28 *"apostles, prophets, teachers, workers of miracles, those having gifts of healings, those able to help others, those with gifts of administration, and those speaking in different kinds of tongues."* They are all equally needed and equally placed there by the Holy Spirit. We need Spirit-filled believers at the church door as well as in the pulpit.

God's formula is the Spirit-filled church, representing the Spirit-filled Jesus on earth. God's plan for his work of expansion and help is by his Spirit. The communion table words are that we "remember him till he comes", "remembering him" as someone who is absent but who will return, but also as one who is always present by his Spirit. We have his presence by the simple act of faith, not by breaking through spiritual barriers to get to him. So much of what transpires within church walls seems like "seeking God" as if God were lost to us and we need to find him. But the Holy Spirit awaits the Word and will show himself whenever the Word is proclaimed.

The gracious words of Jesus, his compassion, his healing hands, his love, his patience as a teacher, his immoveable character – the world needs that Jesus. By the Holy Spirit he can still be heard and encountered – with all his grace and healing – in the Church. We are his voice, his eyes, his feet, his hands, while we have his Holy Spirit actuating our efforts. *"'Neither by might nor by power, but my Spirit,' says the Lord Almighty"* (Zechariah 4:6).

Speaking in Tongues

Part 1

Karen, 17, understood what the baptism in the Spirit was. She was attending a Christian conference and was sitting in a service when the Holy Spirit came upon her, an experience like nothing else she had ever known. Hardly realizing what was happening, she began speaking in tongues. She had not just been hearing about it or receiving instruction that day. She was expecting the Holy Spirit but not particularly at that precise moment. It was God's timing, by grace, a sovereign act of God. Karen spoke in tongues rather than English all that day and the next. Today, over twenty years later, she is a businesswoman, a mother of a fine family, a member of a large church, and is a dynamic worker, truly anointed, and an outstanding department head, touching hundreds of lives.

George was sitting with 150 people in a Communion service. The godly pastor gave a prophetic word: "When you partake of the emblems of Christ, you will be filled with the Spirit and will become a polished shaft in God's quiver." George, aged 14, from a very poor background, knew God had spoken this to him and to him alone. Taking the bread he became aware of the overwhelming presence and power of God and knelt down, weeping with the emotion of the moment. The church service was very quiet. Worried about disturbing it, he put a handkerchief in his mouth. His mother, who was sitting next to him, told him, "George, take your handkerchief out of your mouth." And that is what he did. At once he began to speak fluently in a language unknown to him and in prayer he continued the next day. Besides releasing the gift of tongues, God made it known to him that he was chosen for special service. A lifetime has passed and God blessed him with many talents and gifts. He has served God around the world in multi-capacities, and has reached uncounted thousands for God. That is the baptism in the Spirit.

Wonderful experiences but they are far from isolated cases: Millions today can give similar testimonies, as no doubt many could in the past. The promise is clear in Scripture; it is even a command: *"Be filled with the Spirit"* (Ephesians 5:18). Those instructions are for believers, not the ungodly. Every Christian on earth should be and can be filled with the Holy Spirit. Without the Holy Spirit, religious faith runs on a flat battery. Power from God **is** available.

The insignia of the Spirit in this global revival is *"speaking in tongues"* (Greek *glossolalia*). It is not a new "fad" or "a cult-thing for the brainwashed." It is normal Bible Christianity backed by sound theology and scholarship. The apostle Paul said he spoke in tongues more than anybody (1 Corinthians 14:18). It was standard practice, nothing unusual, in the early church.

In the New Testament the Holy Spirit is always linked with ecstatic manifestations. When such tangible evidence was absent, it was taken as proof that people had not received the Spirit. The first

European convert was Cornelius in Caesarea. He and everyone who heard the gospel with him were baptized in the Spirit and spoke in tongues. This was taken by the apostles as the proof that the Gentiles were accepted by God.

In Austria and France Holy Spirit churches are regarded as a "cult." The early church believers were Holy Spirit people, exactly the same. Were they a "cult"? Pentecostals number 250 million and there are as many charismatics. Their numbers are increasing daily making the Pentecostal-charismatic grouping the second largest Christian group in the world! Quite some cult! Nine out of every ten new Christians belong to this group, whatever their denominational affiliation. It continues with the greatest gospel ingathering to the Kingdom of God ever known. Ninety percent of the increase derives from the baptism in the Holy Spirit with signs following.

The experience is real. It brings those who have it assurance of God's unfailing support in their witness. He is at their elbow. Their expectations do not rest on their own spiritual prowess to attract the power of the Holy Spirit but in God's own faithfulness. This, too, is just as it was in the early days of the church: *"Why do you stare at us as if by our own power or godliness we had made this man walk?"* Peter said. *"The God of our fathers has glorified his servant Jesus"* (Acts 3:12-13). The performer is the Holy Spirit, now shaking nations.

Our own international campaigns are not conducted without the support of all – or at least most of – the different churches in the area. Meetings draw together a sea of people reaching as far as the eye can see, leaving cities empty. While this chapter was being written in August 2006, a campaign was being conducted that was much smaller than usual, the city (Wukari in Nigeria) having a population of only 160,000. In Lagos numbers attending the meetings surpassed the million mark. For 25 years, in addition to the main public services, we have been holding Fire Conferences during the daytime to train and inspire Christian workers for soul-winning. Hundreds of times God has broken into these meetings with mass baptisms in the Holy Spirit, with hundreds and thousands of people speaking in tongues all at once at the same time in a hell-shaking roar of praise. I can say before God that I have experienced over one million people received the baptism into the Holy Spirit within three minutes. *"My Spirit on all people"* (Acts 2:17; Joel 2:28) keeps ringing in my heart.

Part 2

> The fire of the Spirit is falling, the fire ignites everything it touches, and it is spreading as a holy conflagration across continents.

Joel the prophet, who lived several centuries before Christ, made a statement that would then have seemed then like wild ravings: *"I will pour out my Spirit on all people. Even on my servants, both men and women, I will pour out my Spirit in those days"* (Joel 2:28-29). To Israel, God was on the other side of an immense barrier of laws, rules, rites and ceremonies. The stairway to God was so holy and steep that only the most favored priest could go up it. If Joel had said that men would walk on the moon, it could not have sounded less likely to his hearers then. Nonetheless, God is pouring out his Spirit today just as men really have walked on the moon. That is what we are writing about, something God planned that we are now enjoying. This is Joel's prophecy, the century of the Holy Spirit.

The baptism in the Spirit is neither a spiritual pose nor just a denominational doctrine. We do not learn how to speak in tongues. The baptism is not an achievement. God does it. We are passive recipients of spontaneous grace.

This book, written in 2006, recollects that in wartime and the mid-twentieth century, the whole world seemed marooned in the spiritual doldrums. Then came the "charismatic renewal" as we now call it; it touched every section of the church and was especially notable among Catholic leaders. It started a *"cloud as small as a man's hand"* (1 Kings 18:44) presaging rain. Soon the promised "latter rain" began in floods, matching the language of Joel. The whole Christian world today is being refreshed. Vast harvests are being reaped, people by the acre responding and confessing Christ by the gospel. This is so obviously what Joel foretold. What divine mark can it lack?

A growing prayer movement developed during the 19th century. The second advent of Christ was anticipated by the year 2000 and the 20th century would perhaps be the last century of opportunity for evangelism. Prayer warriors begged God for "revival." They asked for power to carry out global work. We now see how effective their prayers were, for today something is happening that is greater than they could ask or think. The Welsh revival of 1904-1906 was a classic event. People have prayed ever since for another "revival" like that one. It produced perhaps a quarter of a million professions of salvation. The cry for a lifetime has been "Lord, do it again!" It is natural to ask God for a repeat performance of such a wonderful past occasion. However, God has no limits and can have other plans. We fortunate people have been born in times when we can see them unfold.

Today, as already mentioned, the baptism in the Spirit has transformed evangelism and outreach, and we are seeing God saving on a scale never known before. The fire of the Spirit is falling, the fire ignites everything it touches, and it is spreading as a holy conflagration across continents.

> The Father sends the Spirit to make our bodies his temples. Could such a thing take place be as if nothing had happened?

In the ancient world, God was thought of as being too remote for anyone to pretend they knew him at close quarters. Even in Israel if anyone had claimed to be Spirit-baptized they would have been considered deluded or blasphemous. The great and dreadful God of Sinai in close and real personal contact? Paranoia, obviously! We ought to feel some sympathy with such incredulity if we ourselves appreciate the limitless glory of infinite God. We should recognize that the very idea of being baptized in God is pretty awesome, by any standards. But it happens to be God's own personal arrangement. Absolutely wonderful, but absolutely true! We think of stellar space, deep and awful and its wheeling systems. We stand in awe. But … the Holy Spirit that authored them, their Creator, is more overwhelming than his creation.

What reactions can we expect when God comes upon us? Surely something! The Psalms indulges in poetry about God coming from the hiding places of his power: *"Why was it, O sea, that you fled? O Jordan that you turned back, you mountains, that you skipped like rams, you hills, like lambs? Tremble, O earth, at the presence of the Lord, at the presence of the God of Jacob"* (Psalm 114:5-7). The Old Testament calls God the "Fear." We shrink from the Holy One. The wonder is that he comes to us – and as the "Comforter." *"Your gentleness has made me great"* (Psalm 18:35, NKJV). Jesus, lover of us all, said he would send him to us! Us! Any of us, not some hand-picked mortals born with a kind of spiritual silver spoon in their mouth.

Many shake or fall when he comes, or are carried out of themselves with unspeakable emotions. That is hardly surprising. It would be odd if it did not affect human beings like that. When God descended on Sinai the whole mountain mass *"trembled violently"* (Exodus 19:18). The Psalmist said, *"I cried to my God for help; my cry came before him, into his ears. The earth trembled and quaked, because he was angry"* (Psalm 18:6-7).The Holy Spirit is the same Spirit that raised Jesus from the dead by the powers of immortality.

In the old revival accounts, we read of people becoming as if they were drunk, making meaningless cries, animal noises, even barking like dogs, and climbing trees. Some of it was obviously neurotic. God did not directly drive people up trees! Such "revival" scenes have no Biblical precedent, but his presence, the God who created heaven and earth, can be overwhelming. God has used the humblest means to reveal himself. We remember that God spoke to Moses from a humble bush. Why should he not speak through the humblest of people?

The reactions of people being filled with the Spirit have been called "froth." Well, froth comes from an ocean wave. Sometimes the froth has been manufactured, simulated, no real wave and no real froth. When the wave of the Holy Spirit hits a crowd of people, it certainly produces froth – real froth. No one could manufacture anything like it. Critics speak of mass emotion in the old revival crowds, hypnotic pressures and excitement being "catching." This book is not advocating mass hysteria but something that is genuinely real from God, nothing less than the promise of Christ himself. He sends his Spirit and our reactions may be one thing or another but now knowledge of the Word guides us. We are not interested in meaningless cries, because the Holy Spirit gives utterance in other tongues, speech in languages, not mere emotion. *"This is what was spoken by the prophet Joel"* (Acts 2:16).

> Speaking in tongues is where the human and divine wills come together. We can only speak in tongues as the Spirit enables us (Acts 2:4); when we speak, it is a kind of unison.

· The Father sends the Spirit to make our bodies his temples. Could such a thing take place be as if nothing had happened? No trace of it? Does God really invest a man with resurrection life simply to have him sit like a plaster Buddha? Scripture suggests that we can expect something quite different: *"If the Spirit of him who raised Jesus from the dead is living in you, he who raised Christ from the dead will also give life to your mortal bodies through his Spirit, who lives in you!"* (Romans 8:11). *"Life to your mortal bodies"* should show! Especially that kind of life – immortal life! The very expression "baptized with the Spirit" is dynamic. It is not a sacramental gesture by a priest. It is real.

C. S. Lewis points out that we humans have few outlets for strong feeling. We can laugh, cry, shout, weep, and be sick with emotion; Dr. Lewis suggests that speaking in tongues is another emotional outlet. We express ourselves that way and so does the Spirit in us, even *"with groans that words cannot express"* (Romans 8:26). Those utterances bear his hallmark. Surely God would not give a sign that was not extraordinary, that was feeble or unattractive. The phenomenon of *glossolalia* is quite extraordinary, a *rara avis* too outlandish to be a religious invention. It is the kind of thing that we would never hanker after, if God had not promised it first; it simply would not cross our minds. It is God's idea. His thoughts are as far above ours as heaven above earth. He startled Moses with the strange sight of a burning bush. Tongues are typical of what God does, hardly surprising when we are filled with the Holy Spirit.

Part 3

It is easy to understand that some people can have a hang-up about speaking in tongues. It involves surrender to God physically, not just in the heart. Many are happy to do his will, but speaking in tongues is where the human and divine wills come together. We can only speak in tongues as the Spirit enables us (Acts 2:4); when we speak, it is a kind of unison.

Our fallen Adamic nature guards its self-possession strictly. But we belong to God. When we are baptized in the Spirit, we recognize his rights. There might well be an instinctive animal resistance as if this incoming force were an invasion. "This is me. It is my body" is for some of us the automatic response.

We naturally protect our physical ego, but God alone has rights over us. The Spirit giving utterance means God is claiming his rights. We are given the fullest assurance. We may be anxious. Jesus himself was aware of that, which is why he asked, *"Which of you, if his son asks for a fish, will give him a snake?"*, following it with the reassuring words: *"How much more will your Father in heaven give good gifts to them that ask him!"* (Matthew 7:9-11). To resolve any tensions we may have, the whole situation is explained in 1 Corinthians 6:19-20: *"Do you not know that your body is a temple of the Holy Spirit, who is in you, whom you have received from God? You are not your own; you were bought at a price. Therefore honor God with your body."* God is not some kind of sadist, out to make us look ridiculous. Speaking in tongues is just what Paul wrote to the Corinthians, honoring God with our body, allowing his work in us.

Speaking in tongues is a wonderful sign of the fact that we were made for God, not just spiritually but in the fullest human sense. God loves and deals with people, not just souls. Without God we are not what the Creator intended. To be a person as God wanted means being full of him. Conversion, new birth, means we receive the divine nature. He joins himself to us (2 Peter 1:4). Jesus was human and divine, the perfect man. The indwelling Spirit is the perfection of human life. Jesus was one person with two natures. He was not outside the normal. He was the normal man, human and divine, not a freak or a mutation, but the ideal. His incarnation showed us the wonderful possibilities of human nature. God made us for himself to identify himself with us in love. Joined to God we are what we should be. Receiving the Spirit is the consummation of life.

To be filled with the Spirit is an outstandingly wonderful opportunity that was in God's plan from the start. God never forces himself upon us. We can hold back, buttoning ourselves up. That is quenching and grieving the Spirit. We have been set free – from ourselves: *"You are not your own"* (1 Corinthians 6:19). *"Offer your bodies as living sacrifices, holy and pleasing to God – this is your spiritual act of worship"* (Romans 12:1).

Are tongues necessary? Does everyone speak in tongues when they are baptized in the Spirit? This question has hard edges. It was thrashed out with absolute honesty by the Assemblies of God of America many years ago, when fundamental distinctions were being written into their fundamental statement. It has to be admitted that God is sovereign and does not tie himself to particular procedures inviolably, but he is nonetheless the God of faithfulness. The heathen gods were unpredictable and treacherous, but the prophets reminded Israel that the Lord stays true to himself and his promise. God could baptize people without signs following, but we cannot build doctrines on exceptional experience. Similarly, Jesus saved people like Mary Magdalene and Zacchaeus without their having any evangelical knowledge. We are not granted doctrinal authority from God. Our authority is only the Word. It lays down no other evidence of the baptism in the Spirit except speaking in tongues. If God performs the exceptional it is not for us to presume upon it and demand the Spirit without tongues.

If anyone wants it that way, without tongues, they are asking for a throw back to 19th century uncertainties. They needed a sign to be sure the Spirit had come to them. Anyone now who wants the Spirit without such a sign is faced with the same problem they had: How can they know they are Spirit-filled? The baptism is so real that it must show, and it would look as if it had not happened unless there was some substantial evidence. A theological or academic theory is no substitute for the mighty infilling and indwelling of the Spirit. It cannot be incidental; it must be vivid and tremendous. Admittedly, the human race is big; we are not made in the same mold, and experiences vary. Some people who have been baptized in the Spirit may not speak in tongues immediately. The fullness of the Spirit may be claimed by somebody somewhere without proof, but we still want proof according to the Word, evidence that it is what the Word promised.

> God never forces himself upon us. We can hold back, buttoning ourselves up. That is quenching and grieving the Spirit.

However, there is another side of the coin: Not everyone who speaks in tongues has been baptized in the Spirit. To enable us to tell the difference, Paul lays down a guideline: Anyone speaking by the Spirit will not curse Jesus (1 Corinthians 12:3). It must be another spirit. The false, the pretending, or the devil-inspired are not hard to detect. God said that if we ask for good food, he will not give us a stone or a scorpion (Matthew 7:9; Luke 11:12). Prayer to the Father in the name of Jesus is heard and answered only by the Father and the Son.

The revelation of speaking in tongues as the sign of the Spirit changed everything. It has had global effects. It should probably be listed as the most important development in the early 20th century. For the first time, believers had positive assurance. They knew God had invested them with power to witness. New boldness took hold of them. Evangelism took on a new dimension.

It seems so obvious that the baptism in the Spirit must carry a sign. How did people not realize that before? Well, it was not the only thing not understood. God is still the God of wonders, the Lord that heals. Yet that also seemed to escape notice and has little mention in whole theological libraries. In the 19th century the truth of divine healing was already being practiced among evangelicals and holiness groups.

Everyone knew that the Christian faith rested on God doing things, even if those things were not always in evidence. The Church lumped together whatever God was doing for Christians and credited it to something called "grace." Grace was not a person, but a kind of holy power from God. It had a will of its own and acted with divine and sovereign authority, choosing who should be saved and who not, for example. We explained this in chapter 3.

The Pentecostal experience focused on the Holy Spirit, not on grace. Teachings on grace had actually left no place in Church doctrine for the baptism in the Spirit. The "grace tradition" obscured the things of the Spirit. Before the baptism in the Spirit was understood, the Word itself had to be understood. During the 19th century Bible teaching developed in that direction. Truth moves slowly in traditional church circles. Actually, many had experienced the Holy Spirit and spoke in tongues without knowing what it was. The Spirit had to wait people's understanding of the Word.

Not surprisingly something so "new" met with opposition. The tradition of a purely spiritual faith was dug deeply into general belief. To disprove it Bible teachers, such as Benjamin Warfield, the principal of Princeton Theological Seminary, made new Bible interpretations. Arguments were launched against tongues-speakers themselves, who were exhorted "to seek fruit, not gifts." Bible students forgot that Scripture said, *"Do not forbid speaking in tongues. Follow the way of love and eagerly desire spiritual gifts"* (1 Corinthians 14:39; 14:1). Lurid tales of paranoia were copied from book to book. However, the pioneers could not deny their experience although for years they were excluded from Christian participation in churchly events. Church rejection sadly rubbed off even on public attitudes and their witness for Christ compromised. Nonetheless, their experience and the Word left them unshakeable though subdued, isolated and misrepresented.

> The Bible knows nothing about air in a jar, only wind in motion. It knows nothing about the Holy Spirit except in action, in manifestation.

This opposition is interesting. It arose from the attitude that considers the Christian faith mainly as a way to heaven, just souls migrating to heaven. Being Spirit-filled at once physically demonstrated that here was a Christian revolution. God had business with us physically as well as spiritually. To the breadth and length of God's love was added depth, *"the whole gospel for the whole man."*

A sense of unworthiness was a block to assurance of Holy Spirit presence and power. The medieval monks searched their souls so diligently that it became a sin of scrupulosity, not merely bowing their heads but groveling. Many Christian people are similar today. Even the blood of Jesus does not make them clean enough. The mark, even the root of sin remains to be confessed and a life of constant penitence is adopted. Such a strong conviction of unworthiness is hardly conducive of faith. If an Everest of piety had to be climbed to be assured of the Holy Spirit's presence, no wonder few men from those groups become world-shakers. The fact is that the Scripture exhorts us all to *"be filled with the Spirit"* (Ephesians 5:18), implying that was intended to be the common experience of every believer.

The early church of the Bible is so often treated as a perfect Christian role model and Christians today compared with it and seen as lamentably lacking. Is it a sign of holiness to admit spiritual poverty and weakness? Al Whittinghill (Ambassadors for Christ), in answering the question "Why is there no revival?" writes, "Surely every honest person in the Church of the Lord Jesus today must have a deep inner awareness that something is wrong." [1] Do we? They may believe it who teach it. Another Christian periodical, The Herald of His Coming, also carries what is said by Crawford Loritts: "We all carry a stain. No matter how many outpourings we have experienced and how much we write and preach and talk about renewal there is a stain that is constantly there."

We cannot relate to that kind of confession. The Bible assurance is that the blood of Jesus cleanses us utterly. It leaves no trace, no mark behind. We walk with God clothed in his righteousness, not in our own respectability. Unless we know we are clean, we cannot know that the Holy Spirit indwells us. Yet the truth is that we can know, and do know, first by the Word and second by the real experience of God with us.

---

[1] From the article "Why is there no revival?" published on the Ambassadors for Christ website, www.afci-usa.com.

If anyone sees churches in low water, something certainly is wrong, as Al Whittinghill says. It is certainly not how God expects things to be. So what is wrong? It lies very close to the people, their assumption that power and blessing are in proportion to holiness. If the hope of blessing depends on high spiritual qualities then that is faith in man, not God. That is the fatal flaw, the little fox that spoils the vineyard (see Song 2:15). No one is so great that they can expect God's mighty favors. God does not give the Spirit to the self-sufficient, but to the needy.

New Testament epistles assume that living in the fullness of the Spirit is normal experience. Christians in the early days of the faith were as imperfect as we are. The Spirit was with them but not because they were superior mortals. They were Spirit-filled because they needed to be Spirit-filled. To be fit for the Holy Spirit we all need the Holy Spirit.

Among the churches Paul looked after, the Galatians disturbed him more than any other. Yet, even that church was marked by the activity of the Holy Spirit. Paul said so. The trouble was that they were adopting a gospel of law, not grace. Having *"begun with the Spirit,"* with miracles, the Galatians switched to legalism (Galatians 3:3-5). Their attitude is traceable today far and near, Christians trying to attain spiritual heights by laboriously climbing to reach the prize of power or fullness at the end. It ends in a non-Holy Spirit gospel. Paul pleaded with the Galatians to continue with the Spirit, to switch back from rules and regulations, for it was either that or lose virtually everything. That is often the plea Christians need to heed today.

The Holy Spirit will manifest himself. He is here for that purpose. The Spirit is the pneuma, wind or breath of God. We cannot have a still and quiet Holy Spirit. There is no such thing as a wind that does not blow or a breath that is not breathed. The Bible knows nothing about air in a jar, only wind in motion. It knows nothing about the Holy Spirit except in action, in manifestation. God is never inactive, never needs us to prod him into life or to rouse him. We are the sleepy ones, not God. Before Christ the winds of the Spirit were not prevailing; *"the Spirit had not been given"* (John 7:39).

The Spirit can be grieved and quenched, but only if he is present. The world cannot grieve the Spirit, because the Spirit does not reside with the world.

Whatever the Spirit does involves people in one way or another. God does nothing on this earth independently of human agency. That is why he wants us to be Spirit-filled. Planting his Spirit in believers links them into a system with him. They become power points on earth ready for his action and through them he accomplishes his will. They are like spiritual lightning conductors bringing the powers of the heavens down to human experience.

We can stretch out our arms to God on behalf of the entire world. Our prayers may be wordless. Our language may be tears, sighs, or our hands lifted to heaven. Our very presence on earth is God's means of working on earth. What we are by the Spirit and by faith makes it possible for God to do what he wants around the curve of the horizon. Jesus said, *"You are the light of the world"* (Matthew 5:14). One light shines a long way. The only thing we need to do is shine.

God has used the humblest means to reveal himself.

We remember that God spoke to Moses from a humble bush.

Why should he not speak through the humblest of people?

CHAPTER 11

New Encounter

We cannot expect divine revelation to be what we imagine. If it was, there would be no need of divine revelation at all. It is special and needs a special approach – nothing less than the guidance of the author, the Holy Spirit. We have to "discern" the Word (1 Corinthians 2:14). A Scripture text shines with luster when set in its proper context, *"apples of gold in settings of silver"* as Scripture says (Proverbs 25:11). This chapter begins with two or three Scriptures that, in isolation, usually raise a few questions. In their proper context I hope they will be seen as beacons of revelation.

The first passage is John the Baptist's introduction of Jesus: *"After me will come one more powerful than I. I baptize you with water, but he will baptize you with the Holy Spirit"* (Mark 1:7-8). The fact is that Jesus did not baptize anybody with the Holy Spirit while he was on earth. He fulfilled the Baptist's word – but only after his ascension. He baptizes now in the Spirit. That is his divine office today, something that we must accept or be in denial of who he is – the Baptizer in the Spirit.

A second such text is John 7:39: *"Up to that time the Spirit had not been given"* (Greek: "the Spirit was not yet"). Not yet? That is surprising. What about Moses, David, Elijah, Elisha, and the prophets? Micah 3:8 says, *"I am filled with power, with the Spirit of the Lord."* Several times in the book of Judges we come across *"the Spirit of the Lord came upon"* one person or other, Othniel, Gideon, Jephthah, Samson. The books of Samuel describe the Spirit coming upon King Saul, King David and such as the prophet Azariah. The apostle Peter wrote, *"Men spoke from God as they were carried along by the Holy Spirit."* (2 Peter 1:21). Jesus told the disciples that the Spirit was with them but would be in them.

All that, and yet *"the Spirit was not yet"*! 1 Corinthians 12:6 tells us, *"There are different kinds of working, but the same God works all of them in all men."* The first disciples certainly experienced the Holy Spirit in more than one form. The world is full of variety, shape, color, size, odor, big, little, hard, soft – all the handiwork of the Spirit. He is the God that deals with us, the God of variety. Some believe that the Spirit we receive at new birth is all we get, and our work is to keep full. It is hard to think the God of wonders has no more to do than what he does when we first trust Christ. No Holy Spirit experiences, no manifested gifts, no tongues? Surely that cannot be right!

Now there is one important thing to note. The Spirit came upon men in ancient Israel by the will of God, not their own will. They were not asking God for power or to do a particular work. As Jesus said to the disciples, *"You did not choose me, but I chose you and appointed you to go and bear fruit"* (John 15:16). He chose them. If they were waiting to hear his voice, and if they are role models in listening to God, it is odd that Scripture never says so. They were called "out of the blue," and were not seeking him. The Spirit "leaped" on them as the Septuagint (Greek) Old Testament says, the same word as in Acts 3:8 where the cripple who had been healed was "walking and leaping". The work of God does not depend on human initiative but on God's own zeal. Men of old became agents of the Spirit, but not by hammering on the door of heaven or prompting God to work. God has never depended on people volunteering. He calls them, recruits them. When God needs somebody to do something, he does not wait around until someone happens to turn up. He calls someone.

It was just like that on the great day of Pentecost (Acts 2). The downward rush of that wonderful Holy Spirit came when he wanted, promised long before when nobody had any idea what was really meant. The disciples did not choose the moment. God took action at his own leisure. That is characteristic of the Holy Spirit. Jesus said, *"The wind blows wherever it pleases. You hear its sound, but you cannot tell where it comes from or where it is going. So it is with everyone born of the Spirit"* (John 3:8).

It does seem a peculiar notion that ardent prayer should be needed to get God to speak! One of the great Christian truths is the revelation that God speaks. Waiting in prayer straining to hear his voice is a misunderstanding of prayer. It is never put like that in Scripture. Some sincere believers wait

> We cannot expect divine revelation to be what we imagine. If it was, there would be no need of divine revelation at all.

with an open mind. But an open mind is a vacuum drawing in any ideas other than from God, even one's own desires. Promptings of the world, the flesh and the devil also can occupy a mental void.

Let's turn to another "problem" verse: *"Among those born of women there has not risen anyone greater than John the Baptist; yet he who is least in the kingdom of God is greater than he"* (Matthew 11:11).

That is one of the most important verses in the Bible. It is a divine announcement of a fundamental advance in divine affairs. It needs to be understood properly. Jesus first preached, *"The kingdom of God is near"* then subsequently *"the kingdom has come upon you."*

To understand what that really means, we can read, say, Psalm 14: *"The Lord looks down from heaven on the sons of men to see if there are any who understand, any who seek God. All have turned aside"* (Psalm 14:2-3). When composed, that Psalm was literally true.

> The Bible is like a roll-call of God's agents in a Satan-occupied world before God's day of deliverance.

Every nation on earth, without any exception except Israel, was shrouded in a dense religious fog of smoke from the altars of idols. A small flame of light flickered on and off in Israel, but even there most of them never quite washed paganism out of their hair. The great powers of Babylon, Greece and Rome lent their weight to gross uncertainties and superstitions. Socrates, reputed to be the wisest of the Greek thinkers, ended his life saying "Crito, we ought to offer a cock to Asclepius. See to it, and don't forget." Asclepius was a god, supposedly the god of healing.

However, during those dark times, God had some who faithful to him, standing against the tidal sweep of godlessness and corruption. These included men we have just talked about, God-chosen individuals, empowered and commissioned for their task. They maintained contact with God in the surrounding obscurity. They were not baptized in the Spirit and at that time could not be because Jesus had yet to come and rend the heavens for the Spirit to come.

Elements of that world story are echoed in the Nazi occupation of Europe during the years of the Second World War. Communication between Europe and the West ceased – but not quite. British agents with incredible courage filtered behind enemy frontiers and worked along with the underground forces of freedom. They learned enemy plans and also kept hopes alive in an oppressed Europe. They represented the promise of an Allied rescue.

The Bible is like a roll-call of God's agents in a Satan-occupied world before God's day of deliverance. Until Christ came proclaiming the kingdom of God, the whole world lay in the lap of the devil. How had that happened? God had given authority and dominion to Adam and Eve (both) over the whole earth. But the "serpent" (the devil) beguiled them, and dethroned them. They fell into the trap of his schemes, the devil stealing their dominion, reigning instead of them, and even reigning **over** them. Even the Apostle John could say, *"The whole world is under the control of the evil one"* (1 John 5:19).

The earth became the devil's kingdom and he the acknowledged *"prince of this world"* – a title given him even by Jesus himself (John 12:31; 14:30; 16:11). Lucifer's original downfall came when he saw the earth as a glittering prize. He wanted it for himself so that he could sit as god on the throne as *"the god of this age"* (2 Corinthians 4:4). He chose the negative of God's positive, darkness instead of light, wickedness instead of good. Jesus said, *"I saw Satan fall like lightning from heaven"* (Luke 10:18).

Jesus also said, *"All the prophets prophesied till John"* (Matthew 11:13). Then came the great change, Christ Jesus came proclaiming the kingdom of God. Just as Europe had its D-day, when the Allies broke through into Europe bringing victory and freedom, so the coming of Christ, breaking through the Satanic wall, began the new age of deliverance, God's D-day. Ever since then – *"from the days of John the Baptist until now"* – attrition of Satanic dominion has continued, *"the kingdom of heaven has been forcefully advancing"* (Matthew 11:12) – millions have been crossing over into the Kingdom, serving the true King, the King of love.

This sea-change in spiritual affairs means that the Holy Spirit has been released to be active on earth. He was not, but now he is. *"Jesus called the Twelve together and gave them power and authority to drive out all demons and to cure diseases, and he sent them out to preach the kingdom of God and to heal the sick"* (Luke 9:1-2). Adam had lost his dominion to the devil, but Christ now reverses matters and gives dominion over the devil to the humble disciples. With Christ the Kingdom has come, and now we are the masters in the power of the Spirit. The occupying enemy has been defeated. *"The reason the Son of God appeared was to destroy the devil's work"* (1 John 3:8). Similar Scriptures use the word *katargeo*, meaning to "nullify, empty".

So far, the devil is a serpent squirming with its head crushed beneath Christ's heel (Genesis 3:15.) The stage of this world's coming emancipation has been set. *"The end will come, when Christ hands over the kingdom to God the Father after he has destroyed all dominion, authority and power. For he must reign until he has put all his enemies under his feet"* (1 Corinthians 15:24-25).

God committed himself to that day of triumph by giving us his Son, who paid the extreme price for victory. The Cross, that ghastly tree from an earthly wood, swung open the door for the Holy Spirit. He has come to abide here for ever, settle here and do his work. It was a cosmic event in signs, wonders, miracles and most of all in the *"salvation we share,"* as Jude 3 calls it. Jesus said, *"Now the prince of this world will be driven out"* (John 12:31). That is taking place daily in the lives of millions filled with the Holy Spirit.

Today, even more than in Bible days, the reality, presence and power of the Holy Spirit is being demonstrated, unmistakably him. What did not happen before does happen now. What was fruitless and impossible before Christ came is seen now every day. Not only material and physical powers are at work, but salvation powers for the whole man. It was never known in the day of Moses or Elijah. Jesus said, *"Do not be afraid, little flock, for your Father has been pleased to give you the kingdom"* (Luke 12:32). We reign with Christ, the powers of the Kingdom of God disposed upon us – the Holy Spirit, the same that broke in when Jesus proclaimed the coming of the Kingdom.

It is time for all God's baptized people to realize who they are, children of the Kingdom, and to know their potency, to fear nothing, and to become spirits of flame to witness to this world. Satan's shadow still darkens the world but he has only been a mere shadow since Christ came. Christ has given us power over all the tricks of the enemy. Our task is not mere demon hunting, miracle mongering and playing games. The church is not a show business. Demons must indeed be cast out and miracles take place, but as Kingdom people we challenge the world's forces of unbelief and godlessness, darkness and wickedness. We, mere mortals, make up God's squads of troops, his men at arms, his answer, his Kingdom ambassadors, crying, *"Be reconciled to God"* (2 Corinthians 5:20).

CHAPTER 12

When the Spirit moves

A question appears as soon as one opens the Bible. We read: *"The earth was formless and empty, darkness was over the surface of the deep, and the Spirit of God was hovering over the waters"* (Genesis 1:2). What immediately strikes us is that the Spirit of God hovered over the chaos but did not change it. Why was he doing that? Why was he waiting?

It is a practical question for us. When **does** the Holy Spirit go into action? Sermons, discussions, and books, at rock bottom all of them really deal with the general business of the blessing of the Holy Spirit. We are good at finding things that may stop God blessing us – it is easy to find human shortcomings and faults which hinder the movings of God. One can soon put a sermon together about human imperfections and how displeased God can be. But what we really need is positive help from God. This is important for us all, and in this chapter will see what light the Bible sheds. Incidentally, we shall also look at the first question about the Holy Spirit doing nothing while brooding over darkness.

Jesus spoke of a period of darkness when the Spirit would do nothing: *"Night is coming, when no one can work. While I am in the world, I am the light of the world"* (John 9:4) By "work" he meant miracle works; at the time, he was dealing with a blind man and spoke of healing as the work of God. He said no man could do that work, the work of God in the night. He was also speaking of his crucifixion, after which he would no longer be seen in the world except by his disciples. Then the light would have gone out and there would be no more works, healings or miracles.

In other words, when there is no Word, there is no Spirit. The Spirit was with Jesus because he was the Word. The Spirit appeared nowhere when Jesus, the Word, lay in the tomb. Yet the Spirit was hovering over that darkness, and when the Father willed it, the Holy Spirit raised Jesus from death. At present, death still prevails over all the earth, and the Holy Spirit hovers over death's darkness, but the Word is coming and the Spirit will raise the dead according to the will of the Father, who alone knows the day and hour when that will happen (Matthew 24:36). Until the day of Pentecost there was no Holy Spirit in the world except where the Word was spoken. Peter preached the first gospel message which he said was the Word of God living and abiding, and the Holy Spirit cast a net and drew in a great catch. Peter had become a fisher of men.

When Jesus came John could write *"the true light is shining"* (1 John 2:8). Then the time came when Jesus was arrested and *"it was night"* (John 13:30). Judas and his armed gang had to come with lanterns (John 18:3). John noted the symbolism of the moment. The world needs lanterns without the light of Christ. The world has substitutes for the true light – ideas, inventions, philosophies, schemes, and self-effort. Compared to the light of Christ they are only lanterns, substitutes for the truth, the real light. They reject the Word as surely as the world crucified Jesus. In that darkness the Holy Spirit does nothing, works no works, other than for those who walk in the light.

In shadowed Gethsemane Jesus said to his captors, *"This is your hour – when darkness reigns"* (Luke 22:53). From that moment when darkness closed in, the Holy Spirit did no works. Until Christ had risen and ascended the Holy Spirit did nothing in the world. The Spirit operates only in the light of the Word.

When Jesus came into the world, the Holy Spirit also came and was with him. Where Jesus was, there was power. The whole world lay in darkness but when he came, the Gentiles saw a great light. The first disciples went out preaching the Word, and the Holy Spirit owned it and blessed it.

> The Holy Spirit's motivation is always the same thing – to charge the Word with heaven's own electric power.

It has been said that God does nothing without prayer, making prayer the Spirit's signal to act. That could be so, but it is a half-truth. The other half is that the Holy Spirit does nothing without the Word. Let's face it, how much would really happen if it depended on church folk praying?

On many occasions the Spirit moved without great prayer sessions for revival, but he never moves without the Word of the gospel. What the Spirit does, even if he does it independently, reveals what he wants to do, for he would never do anything he did not want to do. There has never been any other sign than that he is good, easily entreated, and gracious. The Holy Spirit's motivation is always the same thing – to charge the Word with heaven's own electric power.

"The sword of the Spirit is the Word of God" (Ephesians 6:17), he has no other weapon. He does not go into action wielding our

philosophies, however brilliant they might seem. The Holy Spirit hovers in the darkness, awaiting the Word and then there is light. No amount of pleading in prayer can put the Spirit into action if there is no Word, no preaching of the gospel.

If we turn to Genesis 1 where we read that the Spirit was hovering over the waters, we see that the next verse is *"God said, 'Let there be light'"* (Genesis 1:3). Then the Spirit went into action. The Word spoke and the Spirit obeyed. John's Gospel begins with a parallel verse: *"In the beginning was the Word. Through him all things were made"* (John 1:1-3). The Word is the voice of the Godhead. The Father wills, the Son (the Word) speaks, and the Holy Spirit acts. It is always like that. The Holy Spirit is the performer of the Father's will in response to the voice of the Word.

> No amount of pleading in prayer can put the Spirit into action if there is no Word, no preaching of the gospel.

That is the essential truth – the Spirit follows the Word and the Word only.

A prime example is found in Ezekiel 37. In a vision God showed the prophet Ezekiel a valley of skeletons, "dry bones" and said, *"Prophesy to these bones and say to them, 'Dry bones, hear the word of the Lord.' So I prophesied as I was commanded. And as I was prophesying there was a noise, a rattling sound. They came to life and stood up on their feet – a vast army"* (Ezekiel 37:4,7,10). The sad state of Israel was like that valley of dead bones, but Israel could live again by the Word. Ezekiel did not pray over the bones. He spoke the Word, prophesied, and the Spirit of God made them into an army.

All prophecy is Spirit and the Word. The Spirit came upon men
of old as they were speaking the Word. The Holy Spirit does not
come to give us a blessing, to get us excited, or give us an emotional experience. Those things certainly do happen, but the objective
of the Spirit is not to make us swoon with joy, but to set us on fire
and bring changes into the world.

Prayer is not enough to rouse a dead church. It needs the power
of the Word imbued with the life of the Spirit. Life comes from
the living Word. What we can do and
what we should do is to preach the
Word. Praying for God to work is fine,

> All prophecy is
> Spirit and the Word.

but praying for him to do what we should be doing is pointless.
We cannot send his Spirit anywhere. He moves with us, and he
is where we are. We cannot pray for God to save souls and bless
people and then wait for something to happen. He sends us with
the Word and the Spirit awaits us. It is our privilege to work for
him, save souls for him. For anyone who thinks they do not have
the strength or power, the Word is their strength and their power.
There are two important things to note: Holy Spirit meetings
without the Word are human meetings, and prayer is not a substitute for the Word.

Christian charismatic gatherings may have a Holy Spirit focus. We
can hardly rule that out, but a church can be given over entirely to
the laying on of hands, prophesying, seeking wonders and signs,
casting out demons, and other physical evidences of life in Christ.
The true Christian church gathers around Jesus, at the foot of the
Cross. The Spirit is bonded to him, that Jesus, to love him and not
just seek him for dramatic and emotional effects. We may try to
generate power in "Holy Ghost meetings" as if a miracle was the

> Praying for God to work is fine, but praying for him to do what we should be doing is pointless.

peak of blessing. Our highest ambition should be to exalt and glorify the name of Jesus. That is the place where the Holy Spirit most loves to be. Jesus is our song, our reason for coming together, and where he is, the Holy Spirit is. We are not just Holy Spirit people but Christians, Jesus people, and the Spirit comes to us for Jesus and in our love and worship of Jesus.

To put the Spirit before the Word is the wrong way round. The Holy Spirit follows the Word. To gain the Holy Spirit's presence the Word is needed. The Spirit is especially concerned with Jesus: *"The Spirit will bring glory to me by taking from what is mine and making it known to you,"* Jesus said (John 16:15). The Holy Spirit does not come with a message about himself, but only about Jesus. The Spirit speaks for him, committed to the Word. He answers prayer in the name of Jesus because Jesus is the Word, and the Holy Spirit follows the Word. The will of the Father is written and is spoken by the Son, the Word, and performed by the Spirit. We achieve nothing any other way.

The Bible is full of this truth. In the Old Testament, for example, God spoke at Sinai. They heard his voice, and the Spirit of God rested on Moses and the elders. In the New Testament Jesus spoke the Word, and the Spirit healed the sick. Jesus said that the Father did the works. He willed what should be done, Jesus spoke, and the Spirit went along with it and performed the wonders. *"God anointed Jesus of Nazareth with the Holy Spirit and power. He went around doing good and healing all who were under the power of the devil"* (Acts 10:38).

Our gospel witness is according to the Word. The Holy Spirit blesses the Word when it is spoken. It attracts the power of the Spirit. That is why the gospel is the power of God. The gospel is spoken. The word "gospel" means "good news" but only when spoken. The gospel is not words in a book sitting on a shelf, but it is power words in our mouth. When it is articulated it carries God's power.

The Bible testifies to itself. It declares it is the Word of God, but its claim can be verified. If the Word and the Spirit go together, it should be noticeable. Psalm 119 is a great exposition about the Word. Several verses make claims that are open to testing. For example verse 50 *"My comfort in my suffering is this: your promise preserves my life"* and verse 93 *"I will never forget your precepts, for by them you have preserved my life." "The law of the Lord is perfect, reviving the soul"* (Psalm 19:7). For 2,000 years these claims have been put to the test and proved true.

Jesus said, *"I tell you the truth, whoever hears my word and believes him who sent me has eternal life. The words I have spoken to you are spirit and they are life"* (John 5:24; 6:63).

"You have been born again, not of perishable seed, but of imperishable, through the living and enduring word of God. The word of the Lord stands for ever" (1 Peter 1:23,25).

These words have stood 2,000 years of testing. The Christian faith is not precepts, instructions or ideas, but a power source for human living. The Word brings life. That is why we are commanded to *"preach the Word"* (2 Timothy 4:2). We are not converting people to a religious system, however much hope it might offer.

The gospel is not a system of rites and religious observances, but a life-changing, living force. The gospel is the Word.

> Holy Spirit meetings without the Word are human meetings, and prayer is not a substitute for the Word.

People may argue about the right religion. Religions offer different ways to God or to something, but Jesus left no such way leading to God. He did not found a religion. He said, *"Come to me!"* (Matthew 11:28). He is what we need, what religions lead to perhaps, but he is our Alpha and Omega, our beginning and our ending, our start and our goal.

It can be argued that this or that religion is better than another, but the gospel offers only one thing – Jesus. He is the only One opening his arms to all people. Does anyone have another Jesus to offer? He is everything. He is what he himself talked about. He said, *"He who believes has everlasting life"* (John 6:47). Jesus is not a religion. He is a Person to meet and live by, the living Word. He is not a messenger from God. He is the Message, what the messengers talked about. There is life in him and that life comes to us through the Word.

Those who are anointed, baptized in the Spirit, can quench or weaken the power by living outside the Word of God. Theology is not the same thing. It is meditating, receiving the "engrafted" Word, living by it, letting faith's hand take these words.

Many have spent agonizing hours in prayer but without any grip in their soul from the Word. It is the commonest claim that revival comes from prayer. It has been often said that each revival can be traced back to someone prevailing in prayer. Has this been authenticated? Somebody is bound to have prayed before any revival because everybody does pray, especially for revival. But there has never yet been a revival without the Word. A typical old-time revival began when someone took the gospel Word where it was not heard and preached it. It brought conviction and conversion. Revival has broken out where the spiritual waters were almost dried up. The gospel Word smites the rock and the waters gush forth and bring life where there was no life.

In the Acts of the Apostles the Word was the yardstick of success. We read that *"the word of God continued to increase and spread"* (Acts 12:24), which meant people receiving the Word. The true object of our work is to plant the seed of the Word. Where the Word is, there is life and growth. Soil produces nothing. The secret is the seed in the soil. The seed is the Word, Jesus said.

> Without the Spirit, a Bible message becomes a lecture, head to head, not heart to heart, arid and waterless.

Jesus told the Scribes and Pharisees that they were in error not knowing the Word of God or the power of God. They had the Word but not the Spirit. They took the Word itself and desiccated it, reduced it to dry formulas and faithless teaching. Without the Spirit, a Bible message becomes a lecture, head to head, not heart to heart, arid and waterless. The Spirit can be quenched in the Word by those handling it. Many know the Bible, but *"without faith it is impossible to please God"* (Hebrew 11:6) and therefore they have no Holy Spirit.

By Word and Spirit we can conquer the world for Christ. These two, God's own living Word and the Holy Spirit, are mighty.

They are our resource, our unfailing aid. *"To the law and to the testimony! If they do not speak according to this word, they have no light of dawn"* (Isaiah 8:20).

CHAPTER 13

Practice in the Spirit

When we are Spirit-anointed, can we do and say anything we like and expect God to back us up? What authority do we have, what actions are right and any wrong?

Being filled with the Holy Spirit is wonderful. Our small hearts are an area for the unthinkable greatness of God. We are microscopic compared with his infinite presence. Our will or wishes, even our "rights" seem of little consequence in the depths of God's all-encompassing will. Yet he has given us the right to speak in his name. That is an awesome relationship, but having his Spirit are we now independent to will whatever we want by the Spirit?

Since ministry is mainly in words, what we say can be of the Holy Spirit or not. Could there be presumption, even arrogance? Or is it all Spirit-blessed, bold and assured?

We are trusted with the things of God, to be faithful, to speak in his name. This is where we are tested for what we really are. What is our attitude? To say we are humble proves we are not – it is just the pride of being humble. Paul said that he judged himself, and so must we. How do we measure up and by what rule?

The only "rule" in handling the things of God is what God is. To act in his name, we need to know him. In Scripture many served God. How did they see and understand him?

If just one occasion could be singled out, it would have to be Isaiah chapter 6, a picture of Isaiah meeting God. He saw the truth about God, and who he would be "working for." It disciplined all Isaiah ever said, shaped his prophetic life and message. What affected Isaiah was that vision. He saw the Lord on a throne, high and lifted up. He was attended by celestial beings of indescribable splendor, living, sinless creatures, but great as they were, close to the Throne even they covered their face and could only cry, *"Holy! Holy! Holy is the Lord"* (Isaiah 6:3).

As for Isaiah himself, his reaction was one of self-loathing: *"Woe to me! I am ruined! For I am a man of unclean lips, and my eyes have seen the King, the Lord Almighty"* (Isaiah 6:5). The sight of God's awesome Being affected all his prophecies. That is why nobody spoke of God like Isaiah. The prophecy of Isaiah brings us a realization of God's unimaginable awe, totally different from anything we know, his thoughts as high as heaven above our thoughts. To him the nations are only a drop in a bucket and all the world's inhabitants like grasshoppers, insects carried on the winds.

> Being filled with the Holy Spirit is wonderful. Our small hearts are an area for the unthinkable greatness of God.

Through Isaiah God speaks of himself as "holy" – *"I am the Lord, and there is no other"* (Isaiah 45:6). We do not know what he is like, as we have nobody with whom to compare him: *"To whom will you compare me?"* (Isaiah 46:5). Over and over he calls himself

"I", and stresses it *"I even I"*, *"I am he."* He said he will not give his glory to another – that is, no other Being can rank alongside him (Isaiah 42:8). The worst temptation for those who serve him is to take glory for themselves for the work of God. God heals, God saves – we do not. We are only instruments in his hands – violins, not the player. If we bring blessing, we are not the blessers to accept adulation as blessers. We are nothing without him.

The kind of knowledge Isaiah had would curb any arrogance. Isaiah did not try to push God around! Nor should we! Calling on God in bold faith – that is one thing. But "Say it, and God will do it?" is definitely another. Who do we think we are! God does not perform at our bidding, and is not waiting in the wings for us to call him to take up a centre stage position.

Can we make an offer of God to anyone? "Have more God, more Holy Spirit"? We all want the best God has for us. The point is, however, that God's best is himself, that loving One. We do not say "I want more husband or wife, more father or mother, more son or daughter." They are people, not commodities, and so it is with God. "More" of God can only mean God having "more" of us, more of our lives, our will, and our love. We know his love more when we love him more.

We are imperfect, but God is fully ours from the moment we come to him; there is nothing in reserve. God is not available in quantities, measured out a pound at a time. God is not something to be accumulated, or collected, a possession to add to our store. Isaiah's vision of God certainly would not leave him thinking in those terms! We need not be pedantic over words, but the fact is that we do hear some people offering to give us more Holy Spirit or more God. Can they give so much of God away as they please, as if weighing out candy and passing it over the counter? Is the majesty of the Almighty disposable?

> The worst temptation for those who serve him is to take glory for themselves for the work of God. God heals, God saves – we do not. We are only instruments in his hands

Some speak of "one baptism and many fillings." Is God the Holy Spirit available as top-up "fillings"? No such word or suggestion is found in the 140 "fill" words in Scripture. When God "pours" himself into us, he is not an element brimming in us as leaky vessels that need to be refilled from time to time. God does not evaporate or wear out. The idea of an ebb and flow or up and down relationship with God or the Spirit is not even hinted at in the Word of God. We may wobble but God does not. He is the rock that never rocks. The Spirit is the eternal Spirit, eternal because of the divine quality of his life in us.

A key verse has been made of Ephesians 5:18. *"Do not get drunk on wine, which leads to debauchery. Instead, be filled with the Spirit."* One interpretation is that we have the choice of being drunk with wine or the Spirit. This does not fit the text, as it is too much wine which makes people drunk. There is no possibility of our ever having too much of God.

Then the verse has been taken to mean that we can be drunk with the Spirit. Let us admit that the effect of God can send us reeling, or prostrate us. But this text is not making the effect of being drunk on wine the equivalent of being drunk with the Spirit. It is to be understood as a contrast –not an analogy – of the Spirit affecting us like alcohol. The Holy Spirit does not affect us like alcohol. People talk about being "high" on God as with drugs. That sounds suspect and the Greek text certainly does not allow that interpretation. Drunkenness, inebriation, does not glorify God. God gives us a *"spirit of power, of love and of self discipline,"* or *"a sound mind"* as the NKJV puts it (2 Timothy 1:7).

The same verse from Ephesians has been quoted as an exhortation to seek God for repeated fillings, pointing to the Greek "be being filled". The Greek verb is a present passive imperative, that is, something we do not do but is done to us. It is a command, an obligation resting on us. So we must see to it that we are being filled, though we cannot fill ourselves. It simply means that we keep ourselves open, in a state in which the Holy Spirit can constantly fill us, and he does. Only he can. That state begins with the baptism of the Holy Spirit. How can you be filled unless you have some of the "substance" in you in the first place?

> There is no such thing as "another Pentecost." The Holy Spirit comes to stay.

That is important truth. To be Spirit-baptized is not a once-for-ever experience, or one that is repeatable. We do not receive some Spirit to last us for a while, and then have to go for a further supply, like making regular trips to the supermarket. There is no such thing as "another Pentecost." The Holy Spirit comes to stay. He does not come in a series of short visits before finally deciding to move in, or in various quantities – that is worse than nonsense. It is a parody of the truth.

Water baptism is over and done with in a few moments. The baptism in the Spirit is vitally different. A man can baptize us in water, but only Christ Jesus can baptize us in the Spirit. No man has that power or right. It always was and remains the divine and exclusive prerogative of Jesus; he alone is the baptizer in the Spirit.

When we become Spirit-filled, it opens the dam, the beginning of a never-ending flow, moment by moment coming into us like a river. The same unending effect is when we are saved. It is the beginning of an eternal process. We can say I was saved, have been saved, am being saved, am saved, and shall be saved, because the life working in us is everlasting, a quality that cannot die. Life cannot be static. The essence of life is an active process. The Spirit is a wind, and always blows or it would not be a wind.

Impartation. The laying-on of hands is Biblical. Jesus speaks of disciples ministering healing by placing their hands on sick people (Mark 16:18). It was common practice and is mentioned in many other Scriptures.[1] This could be called "impartation." Healing usually takes place when one person ministers to another. We impart knowledge, the understanding of the Word and of gospel truth bringing God's blessings on someone. The dictionary definition of "impart" is simply to communicate, to bestow something, and to share. That describes our ministry one to another.

When we lay on hands for healing however, we do not "share" healing even if we are sick ourselves. It might be questioned whether we can say we "bestow" healing. Impartation is being held as a doctrine, that is, spiritual blessings can be conferred

---

[1] Mark 6:5; Luke 4:40, 13:13; Acts 6:6, 8:17-18, 13:3, 19:6, 28:8;
     1 Timothy 4:14; Hebrews 6:2.

by touch of the hand, transmitted from one person to another. This meaning of "impart" is not accepted by most charismatic-Pentecostal people. In church language, laying on of hands is not a sacrament. Spirit-baptized Christians speak of ordinances but not sacraments. The two ordinances of baptism and the Lord's Table are physical acts, not the means of spiritual impartation. God uses them only when faith is operated. A spiritual effect can come only by a spiritual cause, prayer and faith in God.

"Impartation" has another side – imparting the Spirit that is, imparting God. We should impart help, encouragement, wisdom, and other such benefits, and we can give hope and strength, but can we give God? Can we say, "I give you the Spirit?" or even "Receive the Spirit"? Is the Spirit ours to do with what we like and to give or bestow on people? Is God such a common and available asset that we can pass him on at will? Can we dispose of him as we wish? Is Jahveh, the great "I am," waiting for a preacher to give him to somebody? Will God the Almighty slip in here or there as directed by an evangelist or Bible teacher? *"Who has directed the Spirit of the Lord?"* (Isaiah 40:13, NKJV).

> The baptism in the Spirit is the anointing of God and is not transferable, certainly not by physical touch!

Impartation has been articulated in songs about wanting "more of God" or "more Holy Spirit." What kind of God do such expressions conjure up? God puts his blessings and gifts in our hands to distribute to others, but only as God wills it. We have no independent authority. Jesus said, *"Freely you have received, freely give"* (Matthew 10:8). But not everything is ours to give. Where is our authority to give "more of God"? It makes him sound like a

> Mortals have no
> franchise to measure
> God out to whom
> they want.
> We cannot receive
> God from man,
> but only from God.
> He has no distribution
> agents of himself.

disposable commodity! God is a Being, a Person, not an element, and he certainly does not submit to our arrogant directions. To say, "I command you to receive the Spirit" is a command to God, or at least making him a dictator!

We cannot direct God, give people God, or fire, or power to people like we give alms – especially not by merely touching them. Laying our hands on somebody for fire seems rather high and mighty. Spiritual fire is God, not a flame falling from God. It is so important to understand that Jesus and Jesus alone is the baptizer in the Holy Spirit and fire. He proceeds from the Father and Son and comes only in the glory of their will. He died, rose again and ascended to the Father to impart the Spirit and fire to us, that great bestowal. We cannot usurp his holy office and place Holy Spirit fire on anyone.

The baptism in the Spirit is the anointing of God and is not transferable, certainly not by physical touch. To try to transfer spiritual blessing by hand or gesture is a voodoo superstition, not faith. The apostles laid hands on the converted Samaritans and they received the Holy Spirit but they had prayed for that to happen (Acts 8:14-17). The laying on of hands is not an impartation but a prayer gesture.

We have all received the Spirit and no one of us is greater in that respect than another. Nobody has extra Spirit, spare power or fire to "share" with others. Our virgin oil is for our own lamp not others (Matthew 25:7-9). The wife of a prophet came to Elisha and at his instructions filled every available vessel with miracle oil but "shut the door." It was hers alone (2 Kings 4:3-7). Mortals have no franchise to measure God out to whom they want. We cannot receive God from man, but only from God. He has no distribution agents of himself. Our part is to minister, teach, encourage, pray one for another. Some minister in a special capacity, but not in superior power. We can *"carry each other's burdens"* (Galatians 6:2), demonstrate faith, encourage one another in faith, and bring hope from the Word. We are all so little before God that differences among us are hardly noticeable.

That does not mean we have no significance or usefulness. Obviously, we do see fruit for our husbandry. In fact, as we walk humbly before our God we are mighty in him, pulling down strongholds (2 Corinthians 10:4), and bringing Holy Spirit gospel power to bear against the worldly world, this *"wicked and adulterous generation"* (Matthew 12:39). It does mean that the equipment God has given us is designed for our own hand alone. Each of us has a sector in the battle front and our supply lines from God are direct and unbreakable. He does not rely on our getting help third hand. Our Captain never lost a battle and never failed one of his men.

When God "pours" himself into us,

he is not an element brimming in us as leaky vessels

that need to be refilled from time to time.

God does not evaporate or wear out.

CHAPTER 14

Eagerly desire spiritual Gifts?

Spiritual gifts seemed something of a temptation to Corinthians. They evidently exercised them, but Paul said, *"I do not want you to be ignorant about them"* (1 Corinthians 12:1). Clearly, they were ignorant about the gifts or at least needed instruction. Having gifts does not mean we have all knowledge. Since the beginning of the present revival of the Spirit, much has had to be learned, and it is hoped this book is an original contribution.

The Corinthians were competing one with another as to who had the best gifts. Clearly, they *"eagerly desired the greater gifts"* (12:31). The NIV misses the point and translates it as a command, "eagerly desire the greater gifts." The alternative reading corrects it: "You are eagerly desiring the greater gift." That is the sense of the passage.[1] So far, so good. However, the Corinthians were making the gifts a matter of boasting – and perhaps that is where things were beginning to go wrong.

Paul wants them to understand better, and then it leads him to the highest level. He does not discourage the gifts, but adds, "Now I will show you something even greater – love." We cannot boastfully compete about loving, but we should compete in love, loving more than others love. *"Consider others better than yourselves. Do*

---

[1] See Greek footnote: Zeloute de ta Xarismata ta diermeneuousin. Zeloute is imperative or indicative.

nothing out of selfish ambition or vain conceit" (Philippians 2:3).
Paul writes thirteen verses on love ending: *"Now these three
remain: faith, hope and love. But the greatest of these is love"*
(1 Corinthians 13:13). When we reach heaven, and all our questions are answered, we shall see that love is everything. Paul was
the world's greatest theologian, but compacts all he knew in one
word, love. Jesus had a similar approach to the law. The apostle was
not the only learned man of God to talk that way. Karl Barth, one
of the most eminent Bible scholars of the 20th century, summed
up everything he knew by quoting the children's hymn: "Jesus
loves me this I know, for the Bible tells me so."

To covet gifts when we are loveless is to behave like children with
toys. *"When I became a man, I put childish ways behind me. In
your thinking be adults"* (1 Corinthians
13:11; 14:10). The gifts are not childish, and Paul did not put them behind
him. In fact, he said, *"I speak in tongues
more than all of you"* – and was grate-
ful to God for it (1 Corinthians 14:18).
However, we should not rival one another in the things of God;
we are encouraged to grow up.

> Paul was the world's
> greatest theologian,
> but compacts all he
> knew in one word,
> love.

One of the criticisms against Spirit-filled-signs-following claims
has been that it is a boast of being superior to others. I have never
heard anyone guilty of such a thought. The fact is that we all have
different gifts and we did not make them ourselves. We cannot
swagger about anything we ever do. Birds can fly, which ranks
them in that way superior to us earthbound mortals. Yet they cannot boast about being able to fly; it is the way they were made.
What we have is God given, whichever gift is concerned. Those

whom God has blessed with the baptism in the Spirit are not in themselves better people, but just thankful to God for such a gift. We all stand before God on level ground. Paul said, *"I am what I am by the grace of God"* (1 Corinthians 15:10).

Today in this third millennium, we stand amazed at the work of God in the last hundred years since the news came that Christians were speaking in tongues in that rough Los Angeles church. The revival has passed through many dark days, many valleys as well mountain heights, and has seen many changes. God has been at work among his people. But while he is changeless, people are not, not even God's people. The Spirit-anointing witness has passed .through two world wars, the world trade recession, and pressed on in times of religious decline and scholars' critical attitudes. Its growth has demonstrated that this is God at work, without any world leader or nationalist motives. It has made an impact on the whole Christian world. Its power is very evident.

Charismatic renewal

After the Holy Spirit testimony had been established, something new took place, the charismatic renewal movement. It had more than one source, but new spiritual desire came from the Secretary of the World Pentecostal Conference, David du Plessis, who was my esteemed personal friend and also a director on the board of *Christ for all Nations*, USA. He felt called to introduce Holy Spirit matters to leading Catholics and others. He told me himself that Smith Wigglesworth had prophesied over him that he would lead the world's greatest revival. A new hunger for God became apparent in the churches in the late 1960s and early 1970s, and particularly for Holy Spirit gifts. We read of bishops dancing round the altar of St. Paul's church in London and of the "Catholic Pentecostals." Historic churches were flooded with new life, new faith.

The realization that God's gifts were available to all Christians today generated even greater desires. Many wanted a more evident walk with God. It was a spiritual revolution and was evinced in a fresh spirit of worship, joy and freedom. The Holy Spirit gave gifts. Beyond gifts he opened a door to a vista of closer intimacy with God.

This was quite incredible for those who had witnessed to the Spirit's work but known only humiliation all their Christian lives; once scorned, they were now honored. Actually, the movement had become self-conscious about tongues and soft-pedaled free worship. Constant critical pressures against the Holy Spirit people tended to stifle or sober their style. They were often found looking to mainline churches as role models of religious decorum, thinking that perhaps hot gospel evangelism was not the way to gain converts.

Yet that very exuberance was exciting Anglicans, Baptists, Lutherans, Methodists and Brethren. These Christians were full of joy, dancing, clapping, and doing the things Pentecostals were supposed to do but were trying not to do for fear of scorn. In the 1970s Pentecostals took the cue from the charismatics and began to throw off their straitjackets, drink deeply of the wine of the Spirit, and *"put on the garments of praise."*

The charismatic movement has linked churches of every kind, all sharing the desire for Spirit-gifted church life. The charismatic movement "desired spiritual gifts." The classic Pentecostal churches had long enjoyed gifts, but only vocal manifestations, tongues, interpretation and prophecy. Looking at Scripture, charismatics independently brought emphasis upon other manifestations, such as the word of knowledge and gifts of healings – not three but nine gifts listed by Paul in 1 Corinthians.

Practices of the Spirit-filled

The classic Pentecostals had more or less an agreed creed, but there were many side shows, various attachments to the fundamental Holy Spirit truth. Moving across many countries, Holy Spirit teaching could become married to local or national religious habits, as well as giving birth to its own new methods, means, and brands.

What common feature entitles churches to belong to one another? Is there something the same in every single church, marking the Holy Spirit movement? It is unlikely but, incredibly, it happens to be close to the truth. One scholar, world expert Dr. Walter Hollenweger, in his book The Pentecostals, wished to show they had no common denominator but he had to stretch far and wide to find any significant variations. In fact the Holy Spirit has created the unity of a thousand denominations and fellowships even on far-flung continents. It is an example of true ecumenism by the Holy Spirit. To be Spirit-filled is the family badge. Earlier critics belabored the movement for its (alleged) tendency to split, but in fact it was a mark of life, all growth being by cells splitting and multiplying and forming a body of many different parts.

1 Corinthians chapters 12 to 14

true

The Corinthian church situation is not fully known. Corinth was a Roman city but with Greek influences. Their gatherings for worship were very different from the regular church pattern anywhere today. Paul spoke of *"the whole church coming together"* – in one place, although it does not say so (1 Corinthians 14:23). Whether the proceedings were anything like ours, formally organized to a set time and length, is very uncertain. Many of the people were slaves, and it would have been difficult for them to be present at all. The non-slaves and better-off could make a day of it. We know they brought food and had good meals together at Christian gatherings. They were different people from the urbanized congregations of today and much more inclined to do their own thing. In his letter Paul tries to bring some order into affairs and that needs to be understood when applying these Scriptures. They are designed for very different people in very different times and with very different practices.

If we begin to treat spiritual manifestations taking Paul's guidance as law, then as with all law it can be legalistically avoided. For example, if there are to be only three prophecies per service (which Paul does not say), then the service can be officially ended and another begun at once to allow for a further three! *hc*

To be serious, there are some obvious principles behind his regulations for Corinthians gatherings. We ought perhaps to examine them here.

1 Corinthians 14:29: *"The others should weigh carefully what is said."* The issue was not so much about how many prophecies

were given but how to handle them. Paul was anxious on this score; prophecy was not to be ruled out but it was to be tested. *"Do not treat prophecies with contempt. Test everything. Hold on to the good"* (1 Thessalonians 5:20). Prophetical utterances were common, often too glib, with everybody wanting to speak at once, which is why Paul says, *"You can all prophesy in turn"* (1 Corinthians 14:31). (Not just three!) He encouraged prophecy but insisted that any emphatic assertion claimed to be by the Spirit should be subjected to our own personal judgment. Prophecy has been the bitter root of major growths of errors, cults, and divisions even in whole denominations. Often there has been no kind of confirmation, but men and women have appeared and been believed on their word alone.

If anyone stands in a Christian gathering, service, conference, or even where two or three are gathered, and brings a prophecy, it must not be accepted officially without some kind of confirmation. It is not valid for one person to direct a church with a prophecy. When a congregation takes action from a prophecy, they are naive and outside the Word of God. Such prophecies were not accepted in apostolic times.

> If we know the Word thoroughly, we shall see that God never gives mandatory commands or peremptory orders, either by prophecy or any other means. He is a guide, not a drill sergeant.

God gives wisdom and it must be applied to prophecies. When a word of prophecy is given, other people have the right to form their own judgment. The right way to handle prophecy is to test it in some way and then only "hold on to what is good." The word "good" does not include any hint of being legal and binding as if it were the Bible.

Even when the prophesier is a man of God, no prophet is infallible. Agabus said the Jews would bind Paul at Jerusalem, but they did not. It was the Romans who did that. Paul ignored many prophecies that would have diverted him from the road God had shown him.

It is a misuse of the gift to pronounce direction for decision or action. That is never seen in the Acts of the Apostles. These utterances are for God's glory and for edification, rebuke and comfort. The reason is obvious – God does not dictate what we should do, because we are made in his image with a free will. He tests us with blessing but also respects our will and our decision. He reveals nothing about our private affairs, but has promised to bless and prosper whatever we do. There is no promise that God will make our decisions for us. What we do is by our own volition, not by order from God. God does not accept responsibility for what we do.

The other side to this is his promised guidance and that *"the steps of a good man are ordered by the Lord"* (Psalm 37:23). Self-will is different from freedom. How God allows us to step where we will, yet guide us, is no great mystery but a lovely assurance. Of course he cannot guide us at all unless we go. A ship must be under way before it can be steered. We walk, but walk in the Spirit, led by the Spirit. That is a matter of our whole Christian life, prayer, Bible, ministry, fellowship, obedience – belonging to God but still ourselves, under no spiritual or pastoral tyranny, for *"if the Son sets you free, you will be free indeed"* (John 8:36).

It has often happened that a man will tell a woman (or vice versa) that God says they should marry, or that it is by prophecy. This is misuse of spiritual things. It is strange that people almost universally assumed that God has a wife or husband waiting in the wings for them. God has no arranged marriages. We can pray and the Lord will certainly have a hand in the matter. He can be at the wedding and bless everything, but heaven is not a marriage bureau and no marriages are made in heaven. God does not fix us up with partners. All our decisions are subject to judgment. God will not decide for us nor accept blame for what we decide. A bad marriage is our mistake, not his. Coincidences and what someone prophesies are not proper criteria for such an important decision as finding a life partner. Someone giving us "a word from the Lord" on this matter should be treated with great caution and ignored altogether without other confirmation. Marriages like that have too often proved earthly, not heavenly. There is no spiritual shortcut to wisdom and forethought.

If we know the Word thoroughly, we shall see that God never gives mandatory commands or peremptory orders, either by prophecy or any other means. He is a guide, not a drill sergeant. God cannot dictate our lives and at the same time give us free will. It is often said that God has a plan for our lives. Yes, in some ultimate sense, for he is the potter molding us. However, he has no blueprint, no set route or targeted ideal that we must first discover and then follow step by step. The only way he recommends is the way of righteousness. On that road we may make mistakes, stumble or fall many times, but we can be sure of one thing: We are still on the road to glory!

Christianity is the

supernatural operation of the Holy Spirit.

The faith once delivered to the saints is a miracle gospel,

a miracle salvation with physical evidences.

CHAPTER 15

What are the "Gifts"?

Paul does not use the normal words for "gifts," because what he means by "gifts" was something quite specific. He carefully avoids the ordinary word everyone used for "gift" (Greek *doron*).[1] 1 Corinthians 12 does not quite say what we might say about "gifts," or as we usually understand the word.

The chapter begins with "spiritual gifts" but the word "gifts" is not actually in the original Greek text. The word that is actually used means "spiritualities" or "spiritual things," or perhaps "spiritual people."

The special "gift" word is Paul's own term, a word everybody knows – charisma, as in the "charismatic" movement. Paul uses it 100 times in his teachings. Charis means grace – a free, unearned gift. Grace in Scripture is God's favor. He is *"full of grace"* (John 1:14), the God of grace, and comes to us smiling, his arms wide open and his hands full of rich treasures.

The "spiritual gifts" (pneuma) are grace gifts, charismata. There are many other grace gifts. Everything to do with God is by grace. Christ himself is the gift of God's grace. Not all grace gifts are

---

[1] Paul's words for gifts were *pneumatika* and *charismata*. He preferred charismata, but the Corinthians liked to talk about being spiritual (*pneuma*), using expressions from their mystery religions, so Paul gave the words that were familiar to them a Christian meaning to help them understand.

miracle gifts, but all miracle gifts are grace gifts. This word charis is related to chara – joy. The Lord is the God of joy. That is his disposition. The gifts of the Spirit are joy gifts.

Paul lists three activities of the Holy Spirit; gifts, services, workings, all by the same Spirit. (1 Corinthians 12:4-5). Our activities achieve very little unless they are also his activities. Jesus said, *"Apart from me you can do nothing"* (John 15:5).

The gifts of the Spirit are not talents or natural genius. One's natural abilities cannot be called "spiritual gifts." Spiritual gifts are divinely actuated. God can work through any one. He does not give tongues to linguists only, wisdom only to trained counselors, or healing gifts just to doctors. He does not need us to be brilliant. *"From the lips of children and infants you have ordained praise"* (Matthew 21:16). Something similar happens in Acts 2:4. The disciples spoke in tongues as the Spirit enabled them. What God does, he does through us, in our action. If anybody does nothing, God does nothing with them. Nevertheless, he still finds a way to bless the world. If we do not do what he wants, he will find somebody else.

If we read carefully, we find that *"to each one the manifestation of the Spirit is given"* (1 Corinthians 12:7) – not a gift, unless we want to call it a gift of a manifestation, which it is of course. Nine manifestations are listed, though there could be others. Paul liked making lists. He wrote, *"To one there is given through the Spirit the* [manifestation of] *word of wisdom, to another the* [manifestation of] *word of knowledge"* (1 Corinthians 12:8, NKJV). Each utterance is a manifestation. That is what is given.

Nobody can come with a word of knowledge at will, or when asked, unless it is a true manifestation of the Spirit – his will.

> Not all grace gifts are miracle gifts, but all miracle gifts are grace gifts.

Nevertheless, there are ministries, when certain people enjoy certain manifestations more often than others. This could be called a "gift." We read "to one there is given through the Spirit the word of wisdom, to another the word of knowledge." It could be that this one or that one is usually given such words, and that would accord with present-day experience in which certain gifts appear to be associated with certain people. We see that in practice in our churches. It is common for particular individuals to speak in tongues or prophesy more than others in church meetings. This is suggested in the phrase referring to another gift *"to another speaking in different kinds of tongues"* (1 Corinthians 12:10), different languages at different times.

When Paul asks, *"Do all speak in tongues?"* (1 Corinthians 12:30) the simple answer is "yes," normally. Tongues are the specific sign of the Spirit for everybody, not an occasional event, so he does not mean that. In fact he says, *"I would like every one of you to speak in tongues"* (1 Corinthians 14:5). This passage mainly relates to what went on in the Corinthian church, its gatherings, and "gift" of tongues is an utterance at that time.

This is important. The Holy Spirit can give a manifestation to anyone. It may be that someone has a ministry in a certain manifestation, but they have no exclusive gift or right. Certain people may develop a notable ministry of healing by faith, but they do not have an exclusive right to it. God can sometimes bring healing through people who do not exercise such a regular service.

As a ministry, however, it should be recognized. No "gift of heal-ing" is ever mentioned in the Bible; the Spirit gives *"to another gifts of healings"* (1 Corinthians 12:9). This indicates one of the services of verse 5. When anyone is called and dedicated to the ministry of healing, then God acknowledges it. He blesses those who go forward in faith according to his will.

Note something important: The promise is *"To another gifts of healings by the one Spirit"* (1 Corinthians 12:9). The "gifts" are plural and the "healings" plural, mentioned three times. Like all the spiritual or charismatic gifts, these gifts of healings, multiple healings, are manifestations of the Spirit, and obviously through some individual. We speak of the "gift of healing," which is not mentioned in Scripture but, strictly speaking, a healing is a gift to a sick person. For example, John and Peter meeting the cripple at the temple said, *"What I have I give you"* (Acts 3:6). They had a gift for the cripple, his healing, and they gave that gift to the man. Each healing is a gift, a manifestation of the Spirit. We do not exercise the power to heal independently. Each healing is by the will of God, through the faith and service of a believer.

> What God does,
> he does through us,
> in our action.
> If anybody
> does nothing,
> God does nothing
> with them.

Those to whom God chooses to give "gifts" (or manifestations) of healing, like Peter did, can give a healing. But anyone – indeed everyone – can bring healing in the name of Jesus, and indeed should do so as they witness to the unsaved. Our personal witness to the godless can be accompanied by miracle cures, confirming the Word according to Mark 16:15-20.

All manifestations are by the Spirit, and he cannot be pushed or obliged to do anything at all, except according to the Word. (See chapter 11, which deals with the relationship between the Word and the Spirit.) He will not acknowledge extravagant and arrogant attitudes; he responds only to the Word, not to anyone's haughty pronouncements about whatever they want.

No one can give a "gift" to someone else. Gifts are not like that. They are manifestations by the will of God from time to time, and no one can bestow any such thing as manifestations on another. People have been invited to come forward to receive a gift of their choice. Nothing could be less like the whole concept of Scripture about God. God is not sitting at a counter ready to hand over such wonder gifts just as we fancy. They are the operation of the Spirit that made heaven and earth.

There are those who talk about "finding your gift." In this case it means a natural gift or talent, which we can develop for God's glory, whatever it is. But a supernatural gift of the Spirit is very different. We do not need to "find" it, but we can neglect the gift, as Paul warned Timothy. We should exhort one another to "use your gift," not find it, for surely nobody can have a charisma of the Spirit and not know it?

With the gift comes the desire and the opportunity. God does not give gifts like scout's badges. They are for those who serve him and they are fitted for that service. Whatever "gifts," strength, power we need, God will give to us at the gate of the harvest field to which he directs us. He gives according to need and circumstances.

> Each healing is a gift, a manifestation of the Spirit.

> With the gift comes the desire and the opportunity. God does not give gifts like scout's badges. They are for those who serve him and they are fitted for that service.

It is all of him. We go in faith, but we can do nothing except what the Word allows, for the Spirit obeys only the Word.

Christianity is the supernatural operation of the Holy Spirit. The faith once delivered to the saints is a miracle gospel, a miracle salvation with physical evidences. The supernatural is only of the Spirit, and only according to the Word. No matter how we read Scripture, it is impossible to see there a gospel shorn of the supernatural. Jesus was stripped at the Cross. We dare not present a Jesus stripped of his omnipotence, promises and compassion. Crowds can be drawn by hype, advertising, or by programs that leave the Word of God aside and whose only reference to the Cross is a painting on the church wall.

The Word of God is more than a spiritual theory. The Lord knows those who belong to him, those who have turned their backs on iniquity, have chosen not to live hedonistic lives, or turn the church itself into a pleasure house. It is all for Jesus – then Jesus is all for us.

The promise is for us, our children and for all who are far off (Acts 2:39). If we do what the apostles did, we shall get what the apostles got. The favor of God has no favorites.

Notes: _____

Learn how to be an explosive soul-winner!

Get ignited and have a fire kindling your evangelistic skills with 8 easy online lessons. Through Reinhard Bonnke's proven soul-winning experience and tools for evangelism, you will gain valuable insights and learn how to bring the world's lost to Christ.

Here's what the **School of Fire** will teach you:

- The basic principles of imparting the truth about the Fire
- The truth about Salvation
- Evangelism as explained in the Bible
- How to practice global Evangelism
- How to depend on the Holy Spirit
- Proven methods for Discipleship and Follow-up

The **School of Fire** will stir a passion for lost souls in you!

Study at your own pace while our comprehensive testing ensures that you have the skills you need to be an explosive soul-winner!

Register online today at:

www.schooloffire.com

and learn how to spread the fire!

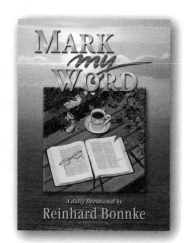

366 DEVOTIONS ONE FOR EVERY DAY OF THE

Mark my Word

"Mark my Word" is a carefully compiled collection of dynamic daily devotionals from the perceptive writings of Evangelist Reinhard Bonnke. Every day you will read sharp, personal, seasoned Biblical insights that have been comprehensively prepared (with thorough scriptural cross-referencing) to help you reap the full benefits from each of the life-changing applications found on every page. You will be enriched and encouraged. In this one volume you'll also discover a wealth of basic Bible background information and inspiration that you'll be able to absorb and apply at your own pace – on a daily basis.

With its simple, convenient, easy-to-read format, you can take this book anywhere and plunge in at any point – choosing to read specific indexed selections focused on a particular topic or category of interest – or read it through and use it as your personal daily devotional, daily Bible reading program, and Bible study guide.

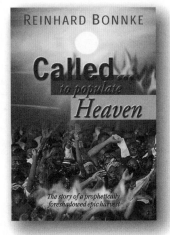

Called to populate Heaven

This is the miraculous story of how over 3.4 million Nigerians found salvation in the city of Lagos, Nigeria, during CfaN's Millennium Crusade. The crusade turned out to be the largest ever held by the organization!

DVD • Widescreen • 60 min. • ISBN 0-9758789-6-4

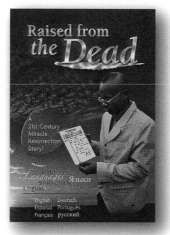

Raised from the Dead

This is the remarkable story of a Nigerian pastor, Daniel Ekechukwu, who was fatally injured in a car accident near the town of Onitsha, Nigeria, Africa on November 30th, 2001. During a dramatic journey to a hospital in Owerri, Nigeria, he lost all life signs and was later pronounced dead by two different medical staff in two different hospitals. The latter wrote a medical report and commissioned the corpse to the mortuary. But Daniel´s wife remembered a verse in Scripture from Hebrews 11:

"Women received their dead raised to life again."

She heard about a meeting where Evangelist Reinhard Bonnke was going to preach, and acted by bringing Daniel´s body in his coffin.
What follows is a story you will never forget.

This DVD contains the following languages:
English, German, French, Spanish, Portuguese and Russian.

DVD • 50 min. per language • ISBN 0-9758789-4-8

PRODUCTIONS
Evangelistic Resources

For ordering Reinhard Bonnke products, please visit our website
www.e-r-productions.com

We also carry a wide range of **products in other languages,**
such as German, Spanish, Portuguese, French ...

Please contact your local office for other languages:

North America & Canada	**Europe**	**Asia & Australia**
E-R Productions LLC	E-R Productions GmbH	E-R Productions Asia Pte Ltd.
P.O. Box 593647	Postfach 60 05 95	451 Joo Chiat Road
Orlando, Florida 32859	60335 Frankfurt am Main	#03-05 Breezeway in Katong
U.S.A.	Germany	Singapore 427664

Latin America	**Southern Africa**	
E-R Productions Ltda	E-R Productions RSA	
Avenida Sete de Setembro	c/o Revival Tape and	
4615, 15 Andar	Book Centre	
Batel, Curitiba – PR	P. O. Box 50015	
80240-000	West Beach, 7449	
Brazil	South Africa	

CfaN CHRIST FOR ALL NATIONS

For CfaN Ministry write to:

North America	**Canada**	**Asia**
Christ for all Nations	Christ for all Nations	Christ for all Nations
P.O. Box 590588	P.O. Box 25057	Asia/Pacific
Orlando, Florida 32859-0588	London, Ontario	Singapore Post Centre
U.S.A.	N6C 6A8	Post Office
		P.O. Box 418
Latin America	**Continental Europe**	Singapore 914014
Christ for all Nations	Christus für alle Nationen	
Caixa Postal 10360	Postfach 60 05 95	**Australia**
Curibita – PR	60335 Frankfurt am Main	Christ for all Nations
80.730-970	Germany	Locked Bag 50
Brazil		Burleigh Town
	United Kingdom	Queensland 4220
Southern Africa	Christ for all Nations	Australia
Christ for all Nations	250 Coombs Road	
P O Box 50015	Halesowen	
West Beach, 7449	West Midlands, B62 8AA	Please visit our website
South Africa	United Kingdom	**www.cfan.org**